Mary Elizabeth Braddon

Lucius Davoren

Vol. I

Mary Elizabeth Braddon

Lucius Davoren
Vol. I

ISBN/EAN: 9783337050702

Printed in Europe, USA, Canada, Australia, Japan

Cover: Foto ©ninafisch / pixelio.de

More available books at **www.hansebooks.com**

LUCIUS DAVOREN

OR

PUBLICANS AND SINNERS

A Novel

BY THE AUTHOR OF
'LADY AUDLEY'S SECRET'
ETC. ETC. ETC.

IN THREE VOLUMES
VOL. I.

LONDON
JOHN MAXWELL AND CO.
4 SHOE LANE, FLEET STREET
1873
[*All rights reserved*]

This Book is Inscribed

TO

VISCOUNT MILTON, M.P. F.R.G.S.
ETC.

IN ACKNOWLEDGMENT OF THE AID DERIVED FROM HIS

ADMIRABLE BOOK OF TRAVELS,

'THE NORTH-WEST PASSAGE OVERLAND,'

TO WHICH THE AUTHOR IS INDEBTED FOR THE

SCENERY IN THE PROLOGUE.

CONTENTS OF VOL. I.

Prologue:—In the Far West.

CHAP.		PAGE
I.	'WHERE THE SUN IS SILENT'	1
II.	'MUSIC HATH CHARMS'	10
III.	HOW THEY LOST THE TRAIL	34
IV.	'ALL'S CHEERLESS, DARK, AND DEADLY'	47
V.	'O, THAT WAY MADNESS LIES'	57

Book the First.

		PAGE
I.	LOOKING BACKWARDS	71
II.	HOMER SIVEWRIGHT	95
III.	HARD HIT	132
IV.	'O WORLD, HOW APT THE POOR ARE TO BE PROUD!'	155
V.	'I HAD A SON, NOW OUTLAW'D FROM MY BLOOD'	171
VI.	'BY HEAVEN, I LOVE THEE BETTER THAN MYSELF'	193
VII.	'SORROW HAS NEED OF FRIENDS'	213

CHAP.		PAGE
VIII.	Geoffrey inclines to Suspicion	227
IX.	Something too much for Gratitude	245
X.	A Daughter's Love, and a Lover's Hope	259
XI.	The Biography of a Scoundrel	270
XII.	Lucius has an Interview with a famous Personage	293
XIII.	He fears his Fate too much	307

LUCIUS DAVOREN

Prologue:—In the Far West.

CHAPTER I.

'WHERE THE SUN IS SILENT.'

WINTER round them: not a winter in city streets, lamplit and glowing, or on a fair English countryside, dotted with cottage-roofs, humble village homes, sending up their incense of blue-gray smoke to the hearth goddess; not the winter of civilisation, with all means and appliances at hand to loosen the grip of the frost fiend: but winter in its bleakest aspect, amid trackless forests, where the trapper walks alone; winter in a solitude so drear that the sound of a human voice seems more strange and awful than the prevailing silence; winter in a pine-forest in British North America, westward of the Rocky Mountains.

It is December, the bleakest, dreariest month in the long winter; for spring is still far off.

Three men sit crouching over the wood-fire in a roughly-built log-hut in the middle of a forest, which seems to stretch away indefinitely into infinite space. The men have trodden that silent region for many a day, and have found no outlet on either side, only here and there a frozen lake, to whose margin, ere the waters were changed to ice, the forest denizens came down to gorge themselves with the small fish that abound there. They are travellers who have penetrated this dismal region for pleasure; yet each moved by a different desire. The first, Lucius Davoren, surgeon, has been impelled by that deep-rooted thirst of knowledge which in some minds is a passion. He wants to know what this strange wild territory is like—this unfamiliar land between Fort Garry and Victoria, across the Rocky Mountains—and if there lies not here a fair road for the English emigrant. He has even cherished the hope of some day pushing his way to the northward, up to the ice-bound shores of the polar sea. He looks upon this trapper-expedition as a mere experimental business, an education for grander things, the explorer's preparatory school.

So much for Lucius Davoren, surgeon without a

practice. Mark him as he sits in his dusky corner by the fire. The hut boasts a couple of windows, but they are only of elk-skin, through which the winter light steals dimly. Mark the strongly-defined profile, the broad forehead, the clear gray eyes. The well-cut mouth and resolute chin are hidden by that bushy untrimmed beard, which stiffens with his frozen breath when he ventures outside the hut; but the broad square forehead, the Saxon type of brow, and clear penetrating eyes, are in themselves all-sufficient indications of the man's character. Here are firmness and patience, or, in one word, the noblest attribute of the human mind—constancy.

On the opposite side of that rude hearth sits Geoffrey Hossack, three years ago an undergraduate at Balliol, great at hammer-throwing and the long jump, doubtful as to divinity exam., and with vague ideas trending towards travel and adventure in the Far West as the easiest solution of *that* difficulty. Young, handsome, ardent, fickle, strong as a lion, gentle as a sucking dove, Geoffrey has been the delight and glory of the band in its sunnier days; he is the one spot of sunlight in the picture now, when the horizon has darkened to so deep a gloom.

The last of the trio is Absalom Schanck, a native of Hamburg, small and plump, with a perennial plumpness which has not suffered even from a diet of mouldy pemmican, and rare meals of buffalo or moose flesh, which has survived intervals of semi-starvation, blank dismal days when there was absolutely nothing for these explorers to eat.

At such trying periods Absalom is wont to wax plaintive, but it is not of turtle or venison he dreams; no vision of callipash or callipee, no mocking simulacrum of a lordly Aberdeen salmon or an aldermanic turbot, no mirage picture of sirloin or Christmas turkey, torments his soul; but his feverish mouth waters for the putrid cabbage and rancid pork of his fatherland; and the sharpest torture which fancy can create for him is the tempting suggestion of a certain boiled sausage which his soul loveth.

He has joined the expedition with half-defined ideas upon the subject of a new company of dealers in skins, to be established beyond the precincts of Hudson's Bay; and not a little influenced by a genuine love of exploration, and a lurking notion that he has in him the stuff that makes a Van Diemen.

From first to last it is, and has been, essentially an amateur expedition. No contribution from the government of any nation has aided these wanderers. They have come, as Geoffrey Hossack forcibly expresses the fact, 'on their own hook.' Geoffrey suggests that they should found a city, by and by, after the manner of classical adventurers: whence should arise in remote future ages some new Empire of the West.

'Hossack's Gate would be rather a good name for it,' he says, between two puffs of his meerschaum; 'and our descendants would doubtless be known as the Hossackides, and the Davorenides, and do their very best to annihilate one another, you know, Lucius.'

'We Chermans have giv more names to blaizes than you Englishers,' chimes in Mr. Schanck with dignity. 'It is our dalend to disgover.'

'I wish you'd disgover something to eat, then, my friend Absalom,' replies the Oxonian irreverently; 'that mouthful of pemmican Lucius doled out to us just now has only served as a whet for my appetite. Like the half-dozen Ostend oysters they give one as the overture to a French dinner.'

'Ah, they are goot the oysders of Osdend,' says Mr. Schanck with a sigh, 'and zo are ze muzzles of Blankenberk. I dreamt ze ozer night I vas in heafen eading muzzles sdewed in *vin de madère*.'

'Don't,' cries Geoffrey emphatically; 'if we begin to talk about eating, we shall go mad, or eat each other. How nice you would be, Schanck, stuffed with chestnuts, and roasted, like a Norfolk turkey dressed French fashion! It's rather a pity that one's friends are reported to be indigestible; but I believe that's merely a fable, designed as a deterring influence. The Maories cannibalised from the beginning of time; fed in and in, as well as bred in and in. One nice old man, a chieftain of Rakiraki, kept a register of his own consumption of prisoners, by means of a row of stones, which, when reckoned up after the old gentleman's demise, amounted to eight hundred and seventy-two: and yet these Maories were a healthy race enough when civilisation looked them up.'

Lucius Davoren takes no heed of this frivolous talk. He is lying on the floor of the log-hut, with a large chart spread under him, studying it intensely, and sticking pins here and there as he pores over it. He has ideas of his own, fixed and definite, which neither of his companions shares in the smallest degree. Hossack has come to these wild regions with an Englishman's unalloyed love of adventure, as well as for a quiet escape from the trusting relatives who would have urged him to go up for Divinity. Schanck has been beguiled hither by the fond expectation of finding himself in a paradise of tame polar bears and silver foxes, who would lie down at his feet, and mutely beseech him to convert them into carriage-rugs. They are waiting for the return of their guide, an Indian, who has gone to hunt for the lost trail, and to make his way back to a far distant fort in quest of provisions. If he should find the journey impossible, or fall dead upon the way, their last hope must perish with the failure of his mission, their one only chance of succour must die with his death.

Very shrunken are the stores which Lucius Davoren guards with jealous care. He doles out each man's meagre portion day by day with a Spartan severity, and a measurement so just that even hunger cannot dispute his administration; the tobacco, that sweet solacer of weary hours, begins to shrink in the barrel, and Geoffrey Hossack's lips linger lovingly over the final puffs of his short black-muzzled meerschaum, with a doleful looking forward to the broad abyss of empty hours which must be bridged over before he refills the bowl. Unless the guide returns with supplies there is hardly any hope that these reckless adventurers will ever reach the broad blue waters of the Pacific, and accomplish the end of that adventurous scheme which brought them to these barren regions. Unless help comes to them in this way, or in some fortuitous fashion, they are doomed to perish. They have considered this fact among themselves many times, sitting huddled together under the low roof of their log-hut, by the feeble glimmer of their lantern.

Of the three wanderers Absalom Schanck is the only experienced traveller. He is a naturalised Englishman, and a captain in the merchant navy; having traded prosperously for some years as the owner of a ship—a sea-carrier in a small way—he had sold his vessel, and built himself a water-side villa at Battersea, half Hamburgian, half nautical in design; a cross between a house in Hamburg and half-a-dozen ships' cabins packed neatly together; everything planned with as strict an economy of space as if the dainty little habitation were destined to put to sea as soon as she was finished. As many shelves and drawers and hatches in the kitchen as in a steward's cabin; stairs winding up the heart of the house, like a companion-ladder; a flat roof, from which Mr. Schanck can see the sunset beyond the westward-lying swamps of Fulham, and which he fondly calls the admiral's poop.

But even this comfortable habitation has palled upon the mind of the professional rover. Dull are those suburban flats to the eye that for twenty years has ranged over the vast and various ocean. Absalom has found the consolation of pipe and case-bottle inadequate; and with speculative ideas of the vaguest nature, has joined Geoffrey Hossack's expedition to the Far West.

CHAPTER II.

'MUSIC HATH CHARMS.'

TEN days go by, empty days of which only Lucius Davoren keeps a record, in a journal which may serve by and by for a history of the ill-fated expedition; which may be found perchance by some luckier sportsmen in years to come, when the ink upon the paper has gone gray and pale, and when the date of each entry has an ancient look, and belongs to a bygone century; nay, when the very fashion of the phrases is obsolete.

Lucius takes note of everything, every cloud in the sky, every red gleam of the aurora, with its ghostly rustling sound, as of phantom trees shaken by the north wind. He finds matter for observation where to the other two there seems only an endless blank, a universe that is emptied of everything except the unvarying pine-trees rising dark against a background of everlasting snow.

Geoffrey Hossack practises hammer-throwing with an iron crowbar, patches the worn-out sleighs, makes little expeditions on his own account, and discovers nothing, except that he has a non-geographical mind, and that, instead of the trapper's unerring instinct, which enables him to travel always in a straight line, he has an unpleasant tendency to describe a circle; prowls about with his gun, and the scanty supply of ammunition which Davoren allows him; makes traps for silver foxes, and has the mortification of seeing his bait devoured by a wolverine, who bears a life as charmed as that Macbeth was promised; and sometimes, but alas too seldom, kills something—a moose, and once a buffalo. O, then what a hunter's feast they have in the thick northern darkness! what a wild orgie seems that rare supper! Their souls expand over the fresh meat; they feel mighty as northern gods, Odin and Thor. Hope rekindles in every breast; the moody silence which has well-nigh grown habitual to them in the gloom of these hungry hopeless days, melts into wild torrents of talk. They are moved with a kind of rapture engendered of this roast flesh, and recognise the truth of Barry Cornwall's dictum, that a poet should be a high feeder.

The grip of the frost-fiend tightens upon them;

the brief days flit by ghostlike, only the long nights linger. They sit in their log-hut in a dreary silence, each man seated on the ground, with his knees drawn up to his chin, and his back against the wall. Were they already dead, and this their sepulchre, they could wear no ghastlier aspect.

They are silent from no sullen humour. Discord has never risen among them. What have they to talk about? Swift impending death, the sharp stings of hunger, the bitterness of an empty tobacco-barrel. Their dumbness is the dumbness of stoics who can suffer and make no moan.

They have not yet come to absolute starvation; there is a little pemmican still, enough to sustain their attenuated thread of life for a few more days. When that is gone, they can see before them nothing but death. The remains of their buffalo has been eaten by the wolves, carefully as they hid it under the snow. The region to which they have pushed their way seems empty of human life—a hyperborean chaos ruled by Death. What hardy wanderer, half-breed or Indian, would venture hither at such a season?

They are sitting thus, mute and statue-like, in the brief interval which they call daylight, when something happens which sets every heart beating with a sudden violence—something so unexpected, that they wait breathless, transfixed by surprise. A voice, a human voice, breaks the dead silence; a wild face, with bright fierce eyes peers in at the entrance of the hut, from which a bony hand has dragged aside the tarpaulin that serves for a screen against the keen northern winds, which creep in round the angle of the rough wooden porch.

The face belongs to neither Indian nor half-breed; it is as white as their own. By the faint light that glimmers through the parchment windows they see it scrutinising them interrogatively, with a piercing scrutiny.

'Explorers?' asks the stranger, 'and Englishmen?'

Yes, they tell him, they are English explorers. Absalom Schanck of course counts as an Englishman.

'Are you sent out by the English government?'

'No, we came on our own hook,' replies Geoffrey Hossack, who is the first to recover from the surprise of the man's appearance, and from a certain half-supernatural awe engendered by his aspect, which has a wild ghastliness, as of a wanderer from the under world. 'But never mind how we came here; what we want is to get away. Don't stand there jawing about our business, but come inside, and drop that tarpaulin behind you. Where have you left your party?'

'Nowhere,' answers the stranger, stepping into the hut, and standing in the midst of them, tall and gaunt, clad in garments that are half Esquimaux, half Indian, and in the last stage of dilapidation, torn mooseskin shoes upon his feet, the livid flesh showing between every rent; 'nowhere. I belong to no party—I'm alone.'

'Alone!' they all exclaim, with a bitter pang of disappointment. They had been ready to welcome this wild creature as the forerunner of succour.

'Yes, I was up some thousand miles northward of this, among icebergs and polar bears and Dog-rib Indians and Esquimaux, with a party of Yankees the summer before last; and served them well, too, for I know some of the Indian lingo, and was able to act as their interpreter. But the expedition was a failure. Unsuccessful men are hard to deal with. In short, we quarrelled, and parted company; they went their way, I went mine. There's no occasion to enter into details. It was winter when I left them—the stores were exhausted, with the exception of a little ammunition. They had their guns, and may have found reindeer or musk oxen, but I don't fancy they can have come to much good. They didn't know the country as well as I do.'

'You have been alone nearly a year?' asks Lucius Davoren, interested in this wild-looking stranger. 'How have you lived during that time?'

'Anyhow,' answers the other with a careless shrug of his bony shoulders. 'Sometimes with the Indians, sometimes with the Esquimaux — they're civil enough to a solitary Englishman, though they hate the Indians like poison — sometimes by myself. As long as I've a charge for my gun I don't much fear starvation, though I've found myself face to face with it a good many times since I parted with my Yankee friends.'

'Do you know this part of the country?'

'No; it's beyond my chart. I shouldn't be here now if I hadn't lost my way. But I suppose, now I am here, you'll give me shelter.'

The three men looked at one another. Hospitality is a noble virtue, and a virtue peculiarly appropriate to the dwellers in remote and savage regions; but hospitality with these men meant a division of their few remaining days of life. And the last of those days might hold the chance of rescue. Who could tell? To share their shrunken stores with this stranger would be a kind of suicide.

Yet the dictates of humanity prevailed. The stranger was not pleasant to look upon, nor especially conciliating in manner; but he was a fellow sufferer, and he must be sheltered.

'Yes,' says Lucius Davoren, 'you are welcome to share what we have. It's not much. A few days' rations.'

The stranger takes a canvas bag from his neck, and flings it into a corner of the hut.

'There's more than a week's food in that,' he says; 'dried reindeer, rather mouldy, but I don't suppose you're very particular.'

'Particular!' cried Geoffrey Hossack, with a groan. '"When I think of the dinners I have turned up my nose at, the saddles of mutton I have despised because life seemed always saddle of mutton, I blush for the iniquity of civilised man. I remember a bottle of French plums and a canister of Presburg biscuits that I left in a cheffonier at Balliol. Of course my scout consumed them. O, would I had those toothsome cates to-day!'

'Balliol!' says the stranger, looking at him curiously. 'So you're a Balliol man, are you?'

There was something strange in the sound of this question from an unkempt savage, with half-bare feet, in ragged mooseskin shoes. The new-comer pushed aside the elf-locks that overhung his forehead, and stared at Geoffrey Hossack as he waited for the answer to his inquiry.

'Yes,' replied Geoffrey with his usual coolness, 'I have had the honour to be gated occasionally by the dons of that college. Are you an Oxford man?'

'Do I look like it?' asks the other, with a harsh laugh. 'I am nothing; I come from nowhere: I have no history, no kith or kin. I fancy I know this kind of life better than you do, and I know how to talk to the natives, which I conclude you don't. If we can hold on till this infernal season is over, and the trappers come this way, I'll be your interpreter, your servant, anything you like.'

'If!' said Lucius gravely. 'I don't think we shall ever see the end of this winter. But you can stay with us, if you please. At the worst, we can die together.'

The stranger gives a shivering sigh, and drops into an angular heap in a corner of the hut.

'It isn't a lively prospect,' he says. 'Death is a gentleman I mean to keep at arm's length as long as I can. I've had to face him often enough, but I've got the best of it so far. Have you used all your tobacco?'

'Every shred,' says Geoffrey Hossack dolefully.

'I smoked my last pipe and bade farewell to the joys of existence three days ago.'

'Smoke another, then,' replies the stranger, taking a leather pouch from his bosom, 'and renew your acquaintance with pleasure.'

'Bless you!' exclaims Geoffrey, clutching the prize. 'Welcome to our tents! I would welcome Beelzebub if he brought me a pipe of tobacco. But if one fills, all fill—that's understood. We are brothers in misfortune, and must share alike.'

'Fill, and be quick about it,' says the stranger. So the three fill their pipes, light them, and their souls float into Elysium on the wings of the seraph tobacco.

The stranger also fills and lights and smokes silently, but not with a paradisiac air, rather with the gloomy aspect of some fallen spirit, to whose lost soul sensuous joys bring no contentment. His large dark eyes—seeming unnaturally large in his haggard face—wander slowly round the walls of the hut, mark the bunks filled with dried prairie grass, and each provided with a buffalo robe. Indications of luxury these. Actual starvation would have reduced the wanderers to boiling down strips of their buffalo skins into an unsavoury soup. Slowly those great wan eyes travel round the hut. Listlessly, yet marking every detail—the hunting knives and fishing tackle hanging against the wall, Geoffrey's handsome collection of rifles, which have been the admiration of every Indian who has ever beheld them. The stranger's gaze lingers upon these, and an envious look glimmers in his eyes. Signs of wealth these. He glances at the three companions, and wonders which is the man who finds the money for the expedition, and owns these guns. There could hardly be three rich fools mad enough to waste life and wealth on such wanderings. He concludes that one is the dupe, the other two adventurers, trading, or hoping to trade, upon his folly. His keen eye lights on Hossack, the man who talked about Balliol. Yes, he has a prosperous stall-fed look. The other, Lucius, has too much intelligence. The little German is too old to spend his substance upon so wild a scheme.

Those observant eyes of the stranger's have nearly completed their circuit, when they suddenly fix themselves, seem visibly to dilate, and kindle with a fire that gives a new look to his face. He sees an object hanging against the wall, to him as far above all the wonders of modern gunnery as the diamonds of Golconda are above splinters of glass.

He points to it with his bony finger, and utters

a strange shrill cry of rapture—the ejaculation of a creature who by long solitude, by hardship and privation, and the wild life of forests and deserts, has lapsed into an almost savage condition.

'A fiddle!' he exclaims, after that shrill scream of delight has melted into a low chuckling laugh. 'It's more than a year since I've seen a fiddle, since I lost mine crossing the McKenzie river. Let me play upon it.'

This in a softer, more human tone than any words he had previously spoken, looking from one to the other of the three men with passionate entreaty.

'What! you play the fiddle, do you?' asked Lucius, emptying the ashes from his pipe with a long sigh of regret.

'It is yours, then?'

'Yes; you can play upon it, if you like. It's a genuine Amati. I have kept it like the apple of my eye.'

'Yes, and it's been uncommonly useful in frightening away the Indians when they've come to torment us for fire-water,' said Geoffrey. 'We tried watering the rum, but that didn't answer. The beggars poured a few drops on the fire, and finding it didn't blaze up, came back and blackguarded us.

I only wish I'd brought a few barrels of turpentine for their benefit. Petroleum would have been still better. *That* would meet their ideas of excellence in spirituous liquors. They like something that scorches their internal economy. They led us a nice life as long as we had any rum; but the violin was too much for them. They're uncommonly fond of their own music, and would sometimes oblige us with a song which lasted all night, but they couldn't stand Davoren's sonatas. Tune up, stranger. I'm rather tired of De Beriot and Spohr and Haydn myself. Perhaps you could oblige us with a nigger melody.'

The stranger waited for no farther invitation, but strode across the narrow hut, and took the violin case from the shelf where it had been carefully bestowed. He laid it on the rough pinewood table, opened it, and gazed fondly on the Amati reposing in its bed of pale-blue velvet; the very case, or outer husk, a work of art.

Lucius watched him as the young mother watches her first baby in the ruthless hands of a stranger. Would he clutch the fiddle by its neck, drag it roughly from its case, at the hazard of dislocation? The surgeon was too much an Englishman to show his alarm, but sat stolid and in agony. No; the unkempt stranger's bony claws spread themselves out gently, and embraced the polished table of the fiddle. He lifted it as the young mother lifts her darling from his dainty cradle; he put it to his shoulder and lowered his chin upon it, as if in a loving caress. His long fingers stretched themselves about the neck; he drew the bow slowly across the strings. O, what rapture even in those experimental notes!

Geoffrey flung a fresh pine-log upon the fire, as if in honour of the coming performance. Absalom sat and dozed, dreaming he was in his cuddy at Battersea, supping upon his beloved sausage. Lucius watched the stranger, with a gaze full of curiosity. He was passionately fond of music, and his violin had been his chief solace in hours of darkest apprehension. Strange to find in this other wanderer mute evidence of the same passion. The man's hand as it hugged the fiddle, the man's face as it bent over the strings, were the index of a passion as deep as, or deeper than, his own. He waited eagerly for the man to play.

Presently there arose in that low hut a long-drawn wailing sound; a minor chord, that seemed like a passionate sob of complaint wrung from a heart newly broken; and with this for his sole prelude the stranger began his theme. What he played, Lucius strove in vain to discover. **His memory could recall no such music.** Wilder, stranger, **more passionate, more** solemn, more awful than **the strain which** Orpheus played **in the** under world, was that music: more demoniac than that diabolical sonata which Tartini pretended to have composed in a dream. **It** seemed extemporaneous, for **it** obeyed none of the laws of harmony, yet even in its discords was scarcely in**harmonious.** There was melody, too, through all— a plaintive under-current of melody, which never **utterly** lost itself, even when the player allowed his **fancy its wildest** flights. The passionate rapture of his haggard, weather-beaten face was reflected in **the** passionate rapture of his music; but it **was not the** rapture of joy; **rather the sharp agony of those convulsions of the** soul which touch the border-line of madness; like the passion of a worshipper at one of those Dionysian festivals in which religious fervour might end in self-slaughter; or like the 'possession' of some Indian devil-dancer, **leaping and wounding** himself under the influence of his demon god.

The three men sat and listened, curiously affected by that strange sonata. Even Absalom Schanck, to whom music was about as familiar a language as the Cuneiform character, felt that this was something out of the common way; that it was grander, if not more beautiful, than those graceful compositions of De Beriot or Rode wherewith Lucius Davoren had been wont to amuse his friends in their desolate solitude.

Upon Lucius the music had a curious effect. At first and for some time he listened with no feeling but the connoisseur's unmixed delight. Of envy his mind was incapable, though music is perhaps the most jealous of the arts, and though he felt this man was infinitely his superior—could bring tones out of the heart of that Amati which no power of his could draw from his beloved instrument.

But as the man played on, new emotions showed themselves upon Lucius Davoren's countenance— wonder, perplexity; then a sudden lighting up of passion. His brows contracted; he watched the stranger with gleaming eyes, breathlessly, waiting for the end of the composition. With the final chord he started up from his seat and confronted the man.

'Were you ever in Hampshire?' he asked, sharply and shortly.

The stranger started ever so slightly at this abrupt interrogatory, but showed no farther sign of discomposure, and laid the fiddle in its case as tenderly as he had taken it thence ten minutes before.

'Hampshire, Massachusetts?' he inquired. 'Yes, many a time.'

'Hampshire in England. Were you in that county in the year '59?' asked Lucius breathlessly, watching the stranger as he spoke.

'I was never in England in my life.'

'Ah,' said Lucius with a long-drawn sigh, which might indicate either disappointment or relief, 'then you're not the man I was **half** inclined to take you **for.** Yet that,' dropping into soliloquy, 'was a **foolish fancy.** There may be more than one man in the world who plays like a devil.'

'You are not particularly complimentary,' returned the stranger, touching the violin strings lightly with the tips of his skeleton **fingers,** repeating the dismal burden of his melody in those pizzacato notes.

'You don't consider it a compliment. Rely upon it, **if Lucifer played the fiddle at** all, he'd play well. The spirit who said, "Evil, be thou my good," would hardly do anything **by** halves. Do you remember what Corelli said to Strengk when he first heard him play? "I have been called Arcangelo, but by heavens, sir, you must be Arcidiavolo." I would give a great deal to have your power over that instrument. Was that your own composition you played just now?'

'I believe **so, or** a reminiscence; but if the latter,

I can't tell you its source. I left off playing by book a long time ago; but I have a reserve fund of acquired music—chiefly German—and I have no doubt I draw upon it occasionally.'

'Yes,' repeated Lucius thoughtfully, 'I should like to play as you do, only—'

'Only what?' asked the stranger.

'I should be inclined to fancy there was something uncomfortable—uncanny, as the Scotch say—lurking in the deep waters of my mind, if my fancies took the shape yours did just now.'

'As for me,' exclaimed Geoffrey, with agreeable candour, 'without wishing either to flatter or upbraid, I can only say that I feel as if I had been listening to a distinguished member of the royal orchestra in Pandemonium—the Paganini of Orcus.'

The stranger laughed—a somewhat harsh and grating cachinnation.

'You don't like minors?' he said.

'I was a minor myself for a long time, and I only object to the species on the score of impecuniosity,' replied Geoffrey. 'O, I beg your pardon; you mean the key. If that composition of yours was minor, I certainly lean to the major. Could you not oblige us with a Christy-minstrel melody to take the taste out of our mouths?'

The stranger deigned no answer to that request, but sat down on the rough log which served Lucius for a seat, and made a kind of settle by the ample fireplace. With lean arms folded and gaze bent upon the fire, he lapsed into thoughtful silence. The blaze of the pine-logs, now showing vivid tinges of green or blue as the resin bubbled from their tough hide, lit up the faces, and gave something of grotesque to each. Seen by this medium, the stranger's face was hardly a pleasant object for contemplation, and was yet singular enough to arrest the gaze of him who looked upon it.

Heaven knows if, with all the aids of civilisation, soap and water, close-cut hair, and carefully-trimmed moustache, the man might not have been ranked handsome. Seen in this dusky hovel, by the changeful light of the pine-logs, that face was grotesque and grim as a study by Gustave Doré; the lines as sharply accentuated, the lights and shadows as vividly contrasted.

The stranger's eyes were of darkest hue; as nearly black as the human eye, or any other eye, ever is: that intensest brown which, when in shadow, looks black, and when the light shines upon it seems to emit a tawny fire, like the ray which flashes from a fine cat's-eye. His forehead was curiously low, the hair growing in a peak between the temples. His nose was long, and a pronounced aquiline. His cheek-bones were rendered prominent by famine. The rest of his face was almost hidden by the thick ragged beard of densest black, through which his white teeth flashed with a hungry look when he talked or smiled. His smile was not a pleasant one.

'If one could imagine his Satanic majesty taking another promenade, like that walk made famous by Porson, and penetrating to these hyperborean shores—and why not, when contrast is ever pleasing?—I should expect to behold him precisely in yonder guise,' mused Geoffrey, as he contemplated their uninvited guest from the opposite side of the hearth. 'But the age has grown matter-of-fact; we no longer believe in the pleasing illusions of our childhood—hobgoblins, Jack and the Beanstalk, and old Nick. Gunpowder and the printing press, as somebody observes, have driven away Robin Goodfellow and the fairies.'

Lucius sat meditative, staring into the fire. That wild minor theme had moved him profoundly, yet it was not so much of the music that he thought as of the man. Five years ago he had heard the description of music—which seemed to him to correspond exactly with this—of an amateur whose playing had the same unearthly, or even diabolical excellence. Certainly that man had been a pianist. And then it was too wild a fancy to conceive for a moment that he had encountered that man, whom he had hunted for all over England, and even out of England, here in this primeval forest. Destiny in her maddest sport could hardly have devised such a hazard. No, the thought was absurd; no doubt an evidence of a brain enfeebled by anxiety and famine. Yet the fancy disturbed him not the less.

'Unless Geoff stalks another buffalo before long, I shall go off my head,' he said to himself.

He brooded upon the stranger's assertion that he was a Southern American, and had never crossed the Atlantic; an assertion at variance with the fact of his accent, which was purely English. Yet Lucius had known American citizens whose English was as pure, and he could scarcely condemn the man as a liar on such ground as this.

'The description of that man's appearance might fit this man,' he thought; 'due allowance being made for the circumstances under which we see him. Tall and dark, with a thin lissom figure, a hooked nose, a hawk's eye; that was the description they gave me at Wykhamston; I had it from three separate people. There is no palpable discrepancy, and yet—bah, I am a fool to think of it! Haven't I had trouble of mind enough upon this score, and would it do any good to her—in her grave, perhaps—if I had my wish: if God gave me the means of keeping the promise I made five years ago, when I was little more than a boy?'

Lucius's thoughts rambled on while the stranger sat beside him, with brooding eyes fixed, like his, upon the flare of the pine-logs.

'By the way,' said Lucius presently, rousing himself from that long reverie, 'when my friend yonder spoke of Balliol, you pricked up your ears as if the name were familiar to you. That's odd, since you have never been in England.'

'I suppose there is nothing especially odd in my having had an English acquaintance in my prosperous days, when even Englishmen were not ashamed to know me. One may be familiar with the name of a college without having seen the college itself. I had a friend who was a student at Balliol.'

'I wonder whether he was the man who wrote "*Aratus sum!*" upon one of the tables in the examiners' room after they ploughed him,' speculated Geoffrey idly.

'I'll tell you what it is, Mr. Stranger,' said

Lucius presently, struggling with **the sense of irritation caused** by that wild fancy which **the** stranger's **playing had inspired,** 'it's all very well **for us to** give you a corner in our **hut.** As good or **evil fortune** brought you this way, we could hardly be **so** unchristian as to refuse you our shelter; God knows **it's poor enough, and death is near** enough inside as well as outside these wooden walls; but even Christianity doesn't oblige us to harbour a man without a **name.** That traveller who fell **among thieves told** the Samaritan his name, rely upon it, as soon as he was able to say anything. No honest man withholds **his name** from the men he breaks bread with. Even the Indians tell us their names; so be good enough to give us yours.'

'**I renounced my own name when** I turned my back upon civilisation,' **answered** the stranger doggedly; 'I brought no card-case to this side of the Rocky Mountains. **If** you give me your hospitality,' with a monosyllabic laugh and a scornful glance **round** the hut, 'solely on condition that I **acquaint** you with my antecedents, I renounce your hospitality. **I can go back to the forest and liberty.** As you say, death could not be much farther off out yonder in the snow. If you only want my name for the purposes of social intercourse, **you** can call me what the

Indians call me, a sobriquet of their own invention, "Matchi Mohkamarn."'

'That means the Evil Knife, I believe,' said Lucius; 'hardly the fittest name to inspire confidence in the minds of a man's acquaintance. But I suppose it must do, since you withhold your real name.'

'I am sure you are welcome to our pasteboards,' said Geoffrey, yawning; 'I have a few yonder in my dressing-bag—rather a superfluous encumbrance by the way, since here one neither dresses nor shaves. But I have occasionally propitiated ravening Indians with the gift of a silver-topped scent-bottle or pomatum-pot, so the bag *has* been useful. Dear, dear, how nice it would be to find oneself back in a world in which there are dressing-bags and dressing-bells, and dinner-bells afterwards! And yet one fancied it so slow, the world of civilisation. Lucius, is it not time for our evening pemmican? Think of the macaroons and rout-cakes we have trampled under our heels in the bear-fights that used to wind up our wine-parties; to think of the anchovy toasts and various devils we have eaten—half from sheer gluttony, half because it was good form—when we were gorged like Strasburg geese awaiting their euthanasia. Think how we have rioted, and wasted and wallowed in what are called the pleasures of the table; and behold us now, hungering for a lump of rancid fat or a tallow-candle, to supply our exhausted systems with heat-giving particles!"

CHAPTER III.

HOW THEY LOST THE TRAIL.

THE slow days pass, but the guide does not return. Geoffrey's sporting explorations have resulted only in a rare bird, hardly a mouthful for one of the four starving men, though they divide the appetising morsel with rigid justice, Lucius dissecting it with his clasp-knife almost as carefully as if it were a subject.

'To think that I should live to dine on a section of wood-partridge without any bread-sauce!' exclaimed Geoffrey dolefully. 'Do you know, when I put the small beast in my bag I was sorely tempted to eat him, feathers and all! Indeed, I think we make a mistake in plucking our game. The feathers would at least be filling. It is the sense of a vacuum from which one suffers most severely; after all it can't matter much what a man puts inside him, so long as he fills the cavity. Do you remember that experimental Frenchman who suggested that a hungry peasantry **should eat** grass? The suggestion was hardly popular, and the mob stuffed the poor wretch's mouth with a handful of his favourite pabulum, when they hung him to a convenient lamp-post **in '93.** But I really think the notion was sensible. If there were a rood of pasture uncovered by the perpetual snow I should imitate Nebuchadnezzar, and **go to** grass!'

Vain lamentations! Vainer still those long argu**ments** by the pine-log fire, in which, with map and compass, they travel over again the journey which has been so disastrous—try back, and find where it was they lost time—how they let slip a day here, half a week there, until the expedition, which should have ended with last September, occupied a period they had never **dreamed of, and** left them in the bleak bitter winter: their trail lost, alone in a trackless forest, the snow rising higher around them day by day, until even the steep bank upon which they have built their log-hut stands but a few feet above the universal level.

From first to last the **journey** has been attended **by** misfortune as **well as mistake.** They had set forth on this perilous enterprise fondly hoping they could combine pleasure for themselves, with profit to their fellow-creatures, and by this wild adventure open up a track for future emigrants—a high road in the days to come from the shores of the Atlantic to the Pacific—a path by which adventurers from the old world should travel across the Rocky Mountains to the gold-fields of the new world. They had started with high hopes—or Lucius had at least cherished this dream above all thought of personal enjoyment —hopes of being reckoned among the golden band of adventurers whose daring has enlarged man's dominion over that wide world God gave him for his heritage—hopes of seeing their names recorded on that grand muster-roll which begins with Hercules, and ends with Livingstone. They had started from Fort Edmonton with three horses, two guides, and a fair outfit; but they had left that point too late in the year, as the guardians of the fort warned them. They were entreated to postpone their attempt till the following summer, but they had already spent one winter in camp between Carlton and Edmonton, and the two young men were resolutely set against farther delay. Absalom Schanck, much more phlegmatic, would have willingly wintered at the fort, where there was good entertainment, and where he could have smoked his pipe and looked out of window at the pine-tops and the snow from one week's end to another, resigned to circumstances, and patiently awaiting remittances from England. But to Lucius Davoren and Geoffrey Hossack the idea of such loss of time was unendurable. They had both seen as much as they cared to see of the trapper's life during the past winter. Both were eager to push on to fresh woods and pastures new, Geoffrey moved by the predatory instincts of the sportsman, Lucius fevered by the less selfish and more ambitious desire to discover that grand highway which he had dreamed of, between the two great oceans. The star which guided his pilgrimage was the lodestar of the discoverer. No idle fancy, no caprice of the moment, could have tempted him aside from the settled purpose of his journey. But a mountain-sheep—the bighorn—or a wild goat, seen high up on some crag against the clear cold sky, was magnet enough to draw Geoffrey twenty miles out of his course.

Of the two guides, one deserted before they had crossed the range, making off quietly with one of their horses—the best, by the way—and leaving them, after a long day and night of wonderment, to the melancholy conviction that they had been cheated. They retraced their way for one day's journey, sent their other guide, an Indian, back some distance in search of the deserter, but with no result. This cost them between three and four days. The man had doubtless gone quietly back to Edmonton. To follow him farther would be altogether to abandon their expedition for this year. The days they had already lost were precious as rubies.

'*En avant!*' exclaimed Geoffrey.

'Excelsior!' cried Lucius.

The German was quiescent. 'I zink you leat me to my deaths,' he said; 'but man must die one time. Gismet, as the Durks say. They are wise beobles, ze Durks.'

The Indian promised to remain faithful, ay, even to death; of which fatal issue these savages think somewhat lightly; life for them mostly signifying hardship and privation, brightened only by rare libations of rum. He was promoted from a secondary position to the front rank, and was now their sole guide. With their cavalcade thus shrunken they pushed bravely on, crossed the mountains by the Yellow Head Pass, looked down from among snow-clad pinnacles upon the Athabasca river, rushing madly between its steep banks, and reached Jasper House, a station of the Hudson's Bay Company, which they found void of all human life, a mere shell or empty simulacrum; in the distance a cheering object to look upon, promising welcome and shelter; and giving neither.

For Hossack, that mighty mountain range, those snow-clad peaks, towering skyward, had an irresistible attraction. He had done a good deal of Alpine climbing in his long vacations, had scaled peaks which few have ever succeeded in surmounting, and had made his name a household word among the Swiss guides, but such a range as this was new to him. Here there was a larger splendour, an infinite beauty. The world which he had looked down upon from Mont Blanc — lakes, valleys, and villages dwarfed by the distance—was a mere tea-board landscape, a toy-shop panorama, compared with this. He drew in his breath and gazed in a dumb rapture,

> ‘Or like stout Cortez, when, with eagle eyes,
> He stared at the Pacific.’

Here, again, they lost considerable time; for even Davoren's stronger mind was beguiled by the glory of that splendid scene. He consented to a week's halt on the margin of the Athabasca, climbed the mountain-steeps with his friend, chased the bighorn with footstep light and daring as the chamois-hunter's; and found himself sometimes, after the keen pleasures of the hunt, with his moccasins in rags, and his naked feet cut and bleeding, a fact of which he had been supremely unconscious so long as the chase lasted. Sometimes, after descending to the lower earth, laden with their quarry, the hunters looked upward and saw the precipices they had trodden, the narrow cornice of rock along which they had run in pursuit of their prey—saw, and shuddered. Had they been really within a hair's-breadth of death?

These were the brightest days of their journey. Their stores were yet ample, and seemed inexhaustible. They feasted on fresh meat nightly; yet, with a laudable prudence, smoked and dried some portion of their prey. In the indulgence of their sporting propensities they squandered a good deal of ammunition. They smoked half-a-dozen pipes of tobacco daily. In a word, they enjoyed the present, with a culpable shortsightedness as to the future.

This delay turned the balance against them. While they loitered, autumn stole on with footstep almost impalpable, in that region of evergreen.

The first sharp frost of early October awakened Lucius to a sense of their folly. He gave the word for the march forward, refusing to listen to Geoffrey's entreaty for one day more—one more wild hunt among those mighty crags between earth and sky.

The sea-captain and Kekek-ooarsis, their Indian guide, had been meritoriously employed during this delay in constructing a raft for the passage of the

Athabasca, at this point a wide lake whose peaceful waters spread themselves amid an amphitheatre of mountains.

While they were getting ready for the passage of the river they were surprised by a party of half-breeds—friendly, but starving. Anxious as they were to husband their resources, humanity compelled them to furnish these hapless wanderers with a meal. In return for this hospitality, the natives gave them some good advice, urging them on no account to trust themselves to the current of the river—a mode of transit which seemed easy and tempting—as it abounded in dangerous rapids. They afforded farther information as to the trail on ahead, and these sons of the old and new world parted, well pleased with one another.

Soon after this began their time of trial and hardship. They had to cross the river many times in their journey—sometimes on rafts, sometimes fording the stream—and often in imminent peril of an abrupt ending of their troubles by drowning. They crossed pleasant oases of green prairie, verdant valleys all abloom with wild flowers, gentian and tiger lilies, cineraria, blue borage—the last-lingering traces of summer's footfall in the sheltered nooks. Sometimes they came upon patches where the forest-trees were blackened by fire, or had fallen among the ashes of the underwood. Sometimes they had to cut their way through the wood, and made slow and painful progress. Sometimes they lost the trail, and only regained it after a day's wasted labour. One of their horses died—the other was reduced to a mere skeleton—so rare had now become the glimpses of pasture. They looked at this spectral equine with sad prophetic eyes, not knowing how long it might be before they would be reduced to the painful necessity of cooking and eating him; and with a doleful foreboding that, when famine brought them to that strait, the faithful steed would be found to consist solely of bone and hide.

So they tramped on laboriously and with a dogged patience till they lost the trail once more; and this time even the Indian's sagacity proved utterly at fault, and all their efforts to regain it were vain. They found themselves in a trackless ring of forest, to them as darksome a circle as the lowest deep in Dante's Inferno, and here beheld the first snow-storm fall white upon the black pine-tops. Here, in one of their vain wanderings in search of the lost track, they came upon a dead Indian, seated stark and ghastly at the foot of a giant pine, draped in his blanket, and bent as if still stooping over the ashes of the fire wherewith he had tried to keep the ebbing life warm in his wasted clay. This gruesome stranger was headless. Famine had wasted him to the very bone; his skin was mere parchment, stretched tightly over the gaunt skeleton; the whitening bones of his horse bestrewed the ground by his side. How he came in that awful condition, what had befallen the missing head, they knew not. Even conjecture was here at fault. But the spectacle struck them with indescribable horror. So too might they be found; the skeleton horse crouched dead at their feet, beside the ashes of the last fire at which their dim eyes had gazed in the final agonies of starvation. This incident made them desperate.

'We are wasting our strength in a useless hunt for the lost track,' said Lucius decisively. 'We have neither the instinct nor the experience of the Indian. Let us make a log-hut here, and wait for the worst quietly, while Kekek-ooarsis searches for the path, or tries to work his way back to the fort to fetch help and food. He will make his way three times as fast when he is unencumbered by us and our incapacity. We may be able to ward off starvation meanwhile with the aid of Geoff's guns. At the worst, we only face death. And since a man can but die once, it is after all only a question of whether we get full or short measure of the wine of life.

> 'And come he slow or come he fast,
> It is but Death who comes at last.'

'Brezisely,' said the Hamburgher. 'It is drue. A man can but die one time—Gismet. Yet ze wine of life is petter zan ze vater of death, in most beoble's obinion.'

Kekek-ooarsis had been absent nearly five weeks at the time of the stranger's appearance, and the length of his absence had variously affected the three men who waited with a gloomy resignation for his return, or the coming of that other stranger, Death. At times, when Geoffrey's gun had not been useless, when they had eaten, and were inclined to take a somewhat cheerful view of their situation, they told each other that he had most likely recovered the lost track at a considerable distance from their hut, and had pushed on to the fort, to procure fresh horses and supplies. They calculated the time such a journey to and fro must take him, allowed a wide margin for accidental delays, and argued that it was not yet too late for the possibility of his return.

'I hope he hasn't cut and run like that other beggar,' said Geoffrey. 'It was rather a risky thing to trust him with our money to buy the horses and provender. Yet it was our only resource.'

'I believe in his honesty,' replied Davoren. 'If he deserts us, Death will be the tempter who lures him away. These Indians have nobler qualities than you are inclined to credit them with. Do you remember that starving creature who came to our hut by the Saskatchewan one day while we were out hunting, and sat by our hearth, famishing amidst plenty, for twelve mortal hours, and did not touch a morsel till we returned and offered him food? I'll forfeit my reputation as a judge of character, if Kekek-ooarsis tries to cheat us. That other fellow was a half-breed.'

'The Greeks weren't half-breeds,' said Geoffrey, whose reading had of late years been chiefly confined to the Greek historians and the more popular of the French novelists, 'yet they were the most treacherous ruffians going. I don't pin my faith on your chivalrous Indian. However, there's no use in contemplating the gloomiest side of the question. Let's take a more lively view of it, and say that he's frozen to death in the pass, with our money intact in his bosom, exactly where you sewed it into his shirt.'

Thus they speculated; the German venturing no opinion, but smoking the only obtainable substitute for tobacco in stolid silence. Indeed, when hard pressed by his companions, he admitted that he had never had any opinion. 'Vat is ze goot ov obinions?' he demanded. 'Man is no petter vor zem, and it is zo much vasted lapour of prain. I do not know how to tink. Zomedimes I have ask my froints vat it is like, tinking. Zey gannot tell me. Zey tink zey tink, put zey to not tink.'

CHAPTER IV.

'ALL'S CHEERLESS, DARK, AND DEADLY.'

The stranger, having had their exact circumstances laid before him, took the gloomiest view of the position. The first deep fall of snow had occurred a week after the guide's departure. If he had not ere that time regained a track, with landmarks familiar to his eye, all hope of his having been able to reach the fort was as foolish as it was vain.

'For myself,' said the stranger, 'I give him up.'

This man, who was henceforth known among them as Matchi, a contraction of the sobriquet bestowed on him by the Indians, fell into his place in that small circle easily enough. They neither liked him nor trusted him. But he had plenty to say for himself, and had a certain originality of thought and language that went some little way towards dispelling the deep gloom that surrounded them. In their wretched position, any one who could bring an element of novelty into their life was welcome. The desperation of his character suited their desperate circumstances. In a civilised country they would have shut their doors in his face. But here, with Death peering in at their threshold, this wild spirit helped them to sustain the horrors of suspense, the dreary foreboding of a fatal end.

But there was one charm in his presence which all felt, even the phlegmatic German. With Lucius Davoren's violin in his hand, he could beguile them into brief forgetfulness of that grisly spectre watching at the door. That passionate music opened the gates of dreamland. Matchi's *répertoire* seemed inexhaustible: but everything he played, even melodies the world knows by heart, bore the stamp of his own genius. Whatever subject of Corelli, or Viotti, or Mozart, or Haydn, formed the groundwork of his theme, the improvisatore sported with the air at pleasure, and interwove his own wild fancies with the original fabric. Much that he played was obviously his own composition, improvised as the bow moved over the strings; wild strains which interpreted the gloom of their surroundings; dismal threnodies in which one heard the soughing of the wind among the snow-laden pine-branches; the howling of wolves at sunrise.

He proved no drone in that little hive, but toiled at such labour as there was to be done with a savage energy which seemed in accord with his half-savage nature. He felled the pine-trunks with his axe, and brought new stores of fuel to the hut. He fetched water from a distant lake, where there was but one corner which the ice had not locked against him. He slept little, and those haggard eyes of his had a strange brightness and vivacity as he sat by the hearth and stared into the fire which his toil had helped to furnish.

Though he talked much at times, but always by fits and starts, it was curious to note how rarely he spoke directly of himself or his past life. Even when Lucius questioned him about his musical education, in what school he had learned, who had been his master, he contrived to evade the question.

'There are some men who have not the knack of learning from other people, but who must be their own teachers,' he said. 'I am one of those. Shut me up in a prison for ten years, with my fiddle for my only companion, and when I come out I shall have discovered a new continent in the world of music.'

'You play other instruments,' hazarded Lucius; 'the cello?'

'I play most stringed instruments,' the other answered carelessly.

'The piano?'

'Yes, I play the piano. A man has fingers; what is there strange in his using them?'

'Nothing; only one wonders that you should be content to hide so many accomplishments in the backwoods.'

Matchi shrugged his lean shoulders.

'There are a thousand various reasons why a man should grow tired of his own particular world,' he said.

'To say nothing of the possibility that a man's own particular world may grow tired of him,' returned Lucius.

Instead of himself and his own affairs — that subject which exalts the most ungifted speaker into eloquence — the stranger spoke of men and manners, the things he had seen from the outside as a mere spectator; the books he had read, and they were legion. Never was a brain stocked with a more heterogeneous collection of ideas. Queer books, out-of-the-way books, had evidently formed his favourite study. Geoffrey heard, and was amused. Lucius heard, and wondered, and rendered to this man that unwilling respect which we give to intellect unallied with the virtues.

Thus three days and nights went by, somewhat

less slowly than the days had gone of late. On the morning of the fourth the stranger grew impatient—paced the narrow bounds of his hut like an imprisoned jaguar.

'Death lies yonder, I doubt not,' he said, pointing to the forest, 'while here there is the possibility—a mere possibility—that we may outlive our troubles; that some luckier band of emigrants may come this way to succour us before we expire. But I tell you frankly, my friends, that I can't stand this sort of life three days longer—to sit down and wait for death, arms folded, without so much as a pipe of tobacco to lull the fever in one's brain. *That* needs a Roman courage which I possess not. I shall not trouble your hospitality much longer.'

'What will you do?' asked Geoffrey.

'Push ahead. I have my chart here,' touching his forehead. 'I shall push on towards the Pacific with no better guide than the stars. I can but perish; better to be frozen to death on the march—like a team of sleigh-dogs I saw once by the Saskatchewan, standing stark and stiff in the snow, as their drivers had left them—than to sit and doze by the fire here till Death comes in his slowest and most hideous shape—death by famine.'

'You had better stay with us and share our

chances,' said Lucius; 'our guide may even yet return.'

'Yes,' answered Matchi, 'at the general muster roll, with the rank and file of the dead.'

His words were strangely belied ere that brief day darkened into night. The four men were sitting huddled round the fire, smoking their final pipe—for Matchi had now shared among them the last remnant of his tobacco—when a curious hollow cry, like the plaintive note of a distressed bird, was heard in the distance.

Lucius was the first to divine its meaning.

'Kekek-ooarsis!' he cried, starting to his feet. 'He has come back at last. Thank God! thank God!'

The call was repeated, this time distinctly human.

'Yes,' said Geoffrey, 'that's the identical flute.'

He ran to the door of the hut. Lucius snatched up one of the blazing pine-branches from the hearth, and went out, waving this fiery brand aloft, and shouting in answer to the Indian's cry. In this moment of glad surprise and hope the man's return meant succour, comfort, plenty. Too soon were they to be undeceived. He emerged from among the shadowy branches, half limping, half crawling towards them across the snow, which was solid enough to bear that light burden without the faintest impression on its frozen surface. He came into the glare of the pine-branch, a wasted ghastly figure, more spectral than their own—the very image and type of famine.

He came back to them empty-handed. No dogs or horses followed him. He came, not to bring them the means of life, but to die with them.

The faithful creature crawled about them like a dog, hugged their knees, laid his wasted body at their feet, looked up at them with supplicating eyes, too feeble for words. They carried him into the hut, put him by the fire, and gave him food, which he devoured like a famished wolf.

Restored by that welcome heat and food, he told them his adventures; how he had striven in vain to regain the track and make his way back to the fort; how, after weary wanderings, he had found himself at last among a little band of Indians, whose camp lay northward of the Englishmen's hut, and who were as near famine as they. Here he had fallen ill with frostbite and rheumatism, but had been kindly succoured by the Indians, not of his tribe. He had lain in one of their shelters—not worthy to be dignified even by the name of hut—for a long time, how long he knew not, having lost consciousness during the period, and thus missed his reckoning. With recovery came the ardent desire to return to them, to show them that he had not betrayed his trust. The bank-notes sewn into his garments had escaped observation and pillage, supposing the Indians inclined to plunder their guest. He asked them to sell him provisions that he might take to his masters, tried to tempt them with liberal offers of payment, but they had unhappily nothing to sell. Buffalo had vanished from that district, the lakes and rivers were frozen. The Indians themselves were living from hand to mouth, and hardly living at all, so meagre was their fare. Convinced at last that the case was hopeless, Kekek-ooarsis had left them to return to the hut—a long and difficult journey, since in his efforts to regain the road to the fort he had made a wide circuit. Only fidelity—the dog's faithful allegiance to the master he loves—had brought him back to that hunger-haunted dwelling.

'I cannot help you,' he said piteously in his native language; 'I have come back to die with you.'

'One more or less to die makes little difference,' answered the stranger, speaking the man's exact dialect with perfect fluency. 'Let us see if we cannot contrive to live. You have failed once in your endeavour to find your way back to the fort. That is no reason you should fail a second time. Few great things have been done at the first attempt. Get your strength back, my friend, and you and I will set out together as soon as you are fit for the journey. I know something of the country; and with your native eyes and ears to help me, we could hardly fail.'

Kekek-ooarsis looked up at him wonderingly. He was not altogether favourably impressed by the stranger's appearance, if one might judge by his own countenance, which expressed doubt and perplexity.

'I will do whatever my masters bid me,' he said submissively.

His masters let him rest, and eat, and bask in the warmth of the pine-logs for two days; after which he declared himself ready to set out upon any quest they might order.

The stranger had talked them into a belief in his intelligence being superior to that of the guide; and they consented to the two setting out together to make a second attempt to find the way to the fort. In a condition so hopeless it seemed to matter very little what they did. Anything was better than sitting, arms folded, as the stranger had said, face to face with death.

But Lucius was now chained to the hut by a new tie. The day after the Indian's return, Geoffrey, the light-hearted, the fearless, had been struck down with fever. Lucius had henceforward no care so absorbing as that which bound him to the side of his friend. The German looked on, phlegmatic but not unsympathising, and made no moan.

'I shall gatch ze fefer aftervarts, no tout,' he said, 'and you vill have dwo do nurse. Hart ubon you.'

CHAPTER V.

'O, THAT WAY MADNESS LIES.'

THE fever raged severely. Delirium held Geoffrey's brain in its hideous thraldom. Horrid sights and scenes pursued him. He looked at his friend's face with blank unseeing eyes, or looked and beheld something that was not there—the countenance of an enemy.

Lucius felt himself now between two fires—disease on one side, famine on the other. Between these two devastators death seemed inevitable. Absalom Schanck, sorely wasted from his native plumpness, sat by the hearth and watched the struggle, resigned to the idea of his own approaching end.

Geoffrey's illness reduced them to a far worse situation than they had been in before, since he was their chief sportsman, and had done much to ward off starvation. Lucius took his gun out for a couple of hours every morning, leaving the invalid in Absalom's charge, and prowled the forest in search of game. But with the exception of one solitary marten, whose tainted flesh had been revolting even to their hunger, his wanderings had been barren of everything but disappointment.

Matchi and the guide had been gone a week, when Lucius set out one morning more desperate than usual, hunger gnawing his entrails, and worse than hunger, a fear that weighed upon his heart like lead—the fear that before many days were gone Geoffrey Hossack would have set forth upon a longer and a darker journey than that they two had started upon together, in the full flush of youth and hope, a year and a half ago. He could not conceal from himself that his friend was in imminent danger—that unless the fever, for which medicine could do so little, abated speedily, all must soon be over. Nor could he conceal from himself another fact—namely, that the stores he had doled out with such a niggard hand would not yield even that scanty allowance for twenty-four hours longer. A sorry frame of mind in which to stalk buffalo or chase the moose!

Again Fortune was unkind. He wandered farther than usual in his determination not to go back empty-handed. He knew but too well that in Geoffrey's desperate state there was nothing his experience could do that Absalom's ignorance could not do as well. In fact there was nothing to be done. **The patient lay in a kind** of stupor. Only the gentle nursing-mother Nature could help him now.

He came upon a circular patch of prairie **in the** heart of the forest, **and** surprised a lean and lonely buffalo, the first he had seen for more than a month. The last had been shot by Geoffrey some days before the guide's departure on his useless journey. The animal was scratching in the snow, trying to get at the scanty herbage under that frozen surface, when Lucius came upon it. His footsteps, noiseless in his moccasins, did not startle the quarry. He stole within easy range, and fired. The first shot hit the animal in the shoulder; then came a desperate chase. The buffalo ran, but feebly. Lucius **fired** his second barrel, this time at still closer quarters, and the brute, gaunt **and** famished like himself, rolled head downwards on the snow.

He took out his hunting-knife, cut out the tongue and choicer morsels, as much as he could carry, and then with infinite labour buried his prey in the snow, meaning to return next **morning with Absalom to** fetch the remainder; provided always that the snow kept his secret, and wolves or wolverines did not devour his prize in the interval. He was able to carry away with him food that would serve for more than a week. No matter how hard or skinny the flesh might be,—it was flesh.

Darkness had closed round him when these labours were finished, but stars shone faintly above the pine-tops: and he carried a pocket-lantern which he could light on emergency. Where was he? That was the first question to be settled. He found some difficulty in recalling the track he had taken. Great Heaven! if he had strayed too far afield, and should find return impossible! Geoffrey yonder dying, without his brotherly arm to support the drooping head, his loving hand to wipe the brow on which the death-damps gathered! The very thought made him desperate. He looked up at the stars, his only guides, shouldered his burden, and walked rapidly in that direction which he supposed the right one.

During their enforced idleness, Geoffrey and Lucius had made themselves tolerably familiar with the aspect of the forest within a radius of ten miles or so from their hut. They knew the course of the river, and its tributary streams. They had even cut rude avenues through the pine-wood, in their quest of fuel, cutting down trees in a straight line at a dozen yards apart, leaving six feet or so of the trunk standing, like a rude pillar; so that within half a mile of their encampment there were on every side certain roughly-marked approaches.

But to-night Lucius had lost ken of the river, and knew himself to be a good ten miles from any tree that he or Geoffrey had ever hewn asunder. He stopped after about half-an-hour's tramp; felt himself at fault; lighted his lantern, and looked about him.

An impenetrable forest; a scene of darksome grandeur, gigantic pine-trees towering skyward, laden with snow; but over all a dreadful monotony, that made the picture gloomy as the shores of Acheron. Nor could Lucius discover any landmark whereby he might steer his course.

He stopped for some minutes, his heart beating heavily. It was not the fear of peril to himself that tormented him. His mind—rarely a prey to selfish fears—was full of his dying friend.

'To be away at such a time!' he thought; 'to have shared all the brightest hours of my youth with him, and not to be near him at the last!'

This was bitter. He pushed on desperately, muttering a brief prayer; telling himself that Heaven could not be so cruel as to sever him from the friend who was dear as a brother, who represented to him all he had ever known of brotherly love.

He paused suddenly, startled by a sight so unexpected that his arm dropped nerveless, and his burden fell at his feet. A light in the thick forest; the welcome glare of a traveller's fire. Not the far-spreading blaze of conflagration, the devouring flames stretching from tree to tree—a spectacle he had seen in the course of his wanderings—but the steady light of a mighty fire of heaped-up pine-logs; a fire to keep wolves and grisly bears at bay, and to defy the blighting presence of the frost-fiend himself.

Lucius resumed his burden, and made straight for the fire. A wide and deep circle, making a kind of basin, had been dug out of the snow. In the centre burned a huge fire, and before it a man lay on his stomach, his chin resting on his folded arms, lazily watching the blazing logs; a man with wild hair and wilder eyes; a man whose haggard face even the red glow of the fire could not brighten.

'What!' cried Lucius, recognising him at the first glance; 'have you got no farther than this, Matchi? A sorry result of your boasted cleverness! Where's the Indian?'

'I don't know,' the other answered shortly. 'Dead, perhaps, before this. We quarrelled and parted two days ago. The man's a knave and a ruffian.'

'I don't believe that,' said Lucius. 'He persevered, I suppose; pushed on towards the fort, and you didn't. That's the meaning of your quarrel.'

'Have it so, if you like,' returned the stranger with scornful carelessness. Then seeing that Lucius still stood upon the edge of the circle—a bank of snow—looking down at him, he lifted his dark eyes slowly, and returned the gaze.

'Have things brightened with you since we parted company?' he asked.

'How should they brighten, unless Providence sent some luckier wanderers across our track?—not a likely event at this time of year. No, the aspect of our affairs has darkened to the deepest gloom. Geoffrey Hossack is dying of fever.'

'Amidst universal cold—strange anomaly!' said the other, in his hard unpitying voice. 'But since death seems inevitable for all of us, I'd gladly change lots with your friend—burn with fever—and go out of this world unconscious. It is looking death in the face that tortures me: to lie here, looking into that fire, and calculate the slow but too swift hours that stand between me and—annihilation. *That* gnaws my vitals.'

Lucius looked down at the strongly-marked passionate face, half in scorn, half in pity.

'You can see no horizon beyond your grave under these pine-trees,' he said. 'You do not look upon this life as an education for the better life that is to succeed it?'

'No. I had done with that fable before I was twenty.'

A hard cruel face, with the red fire shining in it—the face of a man who, knowing himself unfit for heaven, was naturally disposed to unbelief in a future, which for this dark soul could only mean expiation.

'Can you help me to find my way back to the hut?' Lucius asked, after a meditative pause.

'Not I. I thought I was a hundred miles from it. I have been wandering in a circle, I suppose.'

'Evidently. Where did you leave Kekek-ooarsis?'

The stranger looked at him doubtfully, as if hardly understanding the drift of the question. Lucius repeated it.

'I don't know. There is no "where" in this everlasting labyrinth. We disagreed, and parted—somewhere!'

Lucius Davoren's gaze, wandering idly about that sunken circle in the snow, where every inch of ground was fitfully illuminated by the ruddy glare of the pine-logs, was suddenly attracted by an object that provoked his curiosity—a little heap of bones, half burnt, at the edge of the fire. The flame licked them every now and then, as the wind blew it towards them.

'You have had a prize, I see,' he said, pointing to these bones. 'Biggish game! How did you manage without a gun?'

'A knife is sometimes as good as a gun!' said the other, without looking up. He stretched out his long lean arm as he spoke, and pushed the remainder of his prey farther into the fire.

In a moment—before the other was aware—Lucius had leaped down into the circle, and was on his knees, dragging the bones back out of the fire with his naked hands.

'Assassin! devil!' he cried, turning to the stranger with a look of profoundest loathing: 'I thought as much. These are human bones. This is the fore-arm of a man.'

'That's a lie,' the other answered coolly. 'I snared a wolf, and stabbed him with my clasp-knife.'

'I have not worked in the dissecting-room for nothing,' said Lucius quietly. 'Those are human bones. You have staved off death by murder.'

'If I had, it would be no worse than the experience of a hundred shipwrecks,' answered the other, glancing from Lucius to his gun, with an air at once furtive and ferocious, like some savage beast at bay.

'I have half a mind to shoot you down like the wolf you are,' said Lucius, rising slowly from his knees, after throwing the bones back into the blaze.

'Do it, and welcome,' answered the stranger, casting off all reserve with a contemptuous tone, that might be either the indifference of desperation or mere bravado. 'Famine knows no law. I have done only what I daresay you would have done in my situation. We had starved, literally starved—no half rations, but sheer famine—for five days, when I killed him with a sudden stroke of my hatchet. I cut off one arm, and buried the rest of him—yonder, under the snow. I daresay I was half-mad when I did it. Yet it was a mercy to put him out of his misery. If he had been a white skin, I should have tossed up with him which was to go, but I didn't stand on punctilio with a nigger. It may be my turn next, perhaps. Shoot me, and welcome, if you've a mind to waste a charge of powder on so miserable a wretch.'

'No,' said Lucius, 'no one has made me your judge or your executioner. I leave you to your conscience. But if ever you darken the threshold of our hut again—be your errand what it may—by the God above us both, you shall die like a dog!'

Matchi's keen eyes followed the vanishing form

of his accuser, and his thin lips shaped themselves into a triumphant grin.

'You didn't inquire about the money the Indian carried,' he muttered. '*That* was my real motive. Better to be thought a cannibal than a thief. And with that money I can begin life again if ever I get clear of this forest.'

Lucius Davoren spent that night in the forest, by a fire of his own kindling, after having put some distance between himself and that other wanderer. He recruited exhausted nature with a buffalo steak, and then sat out the night by his lonely fire; sometimes dozing, more often watching, knowing not when murder might creep upon him with stealthy footfall across the silent snow. Morning came, however, and the night had brought no attack. By daylight he regained the lost trail, found his way back to the hut, laden with his spoil, and to his unspeakable joy found a change for the better in the sick man.

'I have gaven him his traft, bongdual,' said Mr. Schanck, pointing to the empty medicine bottle, 'and he is gooller; he bersbires. Dat is goot.'

'Von der Stirne heisse,
Rinnen muss der Schweiss.'

Yes, perspiration had arisen, nature's healing

dew; not the awful damps of swift-coming death. Lucius knelt by the rough bed, and thanked God for this happy change. How sweet was prayer at such a moment! He thought of that murderous wretch in the forest, waiting for the death he had sought to defer by famine's last loathsome resource; that revolting expedient which it was horror to think of—a lost wretch without a hope beyond the grave, without belief in a God.

On his knees, his breast swollen by the rapture of gratitude and glad surprise, Lucius thought of that wretch almost with pity.

He made a strong broth with some of the buffalo flesh, and fed his patient by spoonfuls. To rally from such prostration must needs be a slow process; but once hopeful of his friend's recovery, Lucius was content to wait for the issue in quiet confidence.

He told Absalom his adventure in the forest, the hideous discovery of the faithful Indian's fate.

'Vat for a man! And vhen he has digesded the Indian, and feels again vhat boor Geoffrey used to gall a vaguum, he vill gome and ead us,' said the German despondently.

'He will not cross this threshold. What! do you think I would let that ravening beast approach *him ?*' pointing to the prostrate figure on the bed.

'I have told him what I should do if he came here. He knows the penalty.'

'You vould gill him?'

'Without one scruple.'

'I tink you are in your right,' answered Absalom tranquilly. 'It is an onbleasant itea do be eaden.'

Two days passed slowly. Geoffrey rallied. Very slow was the progress towards recovery—almost imperceptible to the non-professional eye, but it was progress. Lucius perceived it, and was thankful. He had not slept since that night in the forest, but watched all night beside the patient's bed—his gun within reach of his hand, loaded with ball.

On the third night of his watch, when Geoffrey had been wandering a little, and then had fallen into a placid slumber, there came a sound at the door—a sound that was neither the waving of a pine-branch nor the cry of bird or beast; a sound distinctly human.

Lucius had barricaded his door with a couple of pine-trunks, placed transversely, like a St. Andrew's cross. The door itself was a fragile contrivance (three or four roughly-hewn planks nailed loosely together), but the St. Andrew's cross made a formidable barrier.

He heard the door tried with a rough impatient hand. The pine-trunks groaned, but held firm. The door was shaken again; then, after a moment's pause, the same impatient hand shook the little parchment window. This offered but a frail defence; it rattled, yielded, then, after one vigorous thrust, burst inward, and a dark ragged head and strong bony shoulders appeared in the opening.

'I am starving,' cried a hoarse voice, faint, yet with a strange force in its hollow tones. It was the voice of the man who called himself Matchi. 'Give me shelter—food—if you have any to give. It is my last chance,' he gasped breathlessly.

He widened the space about him with those strong desperate arms, and made as if he would have leapt into the hut. Lucius raised his gun, cocked it, and took aim deliberately, without an instant's hesitation.

'I told you what would happen if you came here,' he said, and, with the words, fired.

The man fell backwards, dragging the thin parchment window and some part of its fragile framework with him. His death-clutch had fastened on the splintered wood. A wild gust of north-east wind rushed in through the blank space in the log wall, but Lucius Davoren did not feel it.

'Great God!' he asked himself, a slow horror creeping through his ice-cold veins, 'was that a murder?'

END OF THE PROLOGUE.

Book the First.

CHAPTER I.

LOOKING BACKWARDS.

BEHOLD, O reader, the eastern end of the great city; a region strange beyond all measure to the dwellers in the west; a low flat marshy district, where the land and the river seem to have become entangled with each other in inextricable confusion, by reason of manifold creeks and creeklets, basins, and pools, which encroach upon the shore, and where the tall spars of mighty merchantmen and giant emigrant-ships rise cheek by jowl with factory chimneys; where the streets are dark and narrow, and the sound of engines hoarsely labouring greets the ear at every turn; where the staple commodity seems to be ship-biscuit; where the shipchandler has his stronghold; where the provision-dealer has his storehouse, in which vast hoards of dried meats and tinned provisions, pickles, and groceries are piled from floor to ceiling and from cellar to garret; a world in which the explorer stumbles unawares upon rope-walks, or finds himself suddenly involved in a cloud of bonnetless factory girls, thick as locusts in Arabia, who jibe and flout at the stranger. Roads there are, broad and airy enough, which lead away from the narrow streets and the stone basins, the quays, the docks, the steam-cranes, and tall ships—not to the country, there seems no such thing as country accessible from this peculiar world—but to distant marshes and broader water; roads fringed with dingy houses, and here and there a factory, and here and there a house of larger size and greater pretension than its neighbours, shut in by high walls perchance, and boasting an ancient garden; a garden where the tall elms were saplings in the days when kings went hunting on the Essex coast yonder; and when this east-end of London had its share of fashion and splendour.

Perhaps of all these broader thoroughfares, Shadrack-road was the shabbiest. It had struggled into existence later than the rest, and in all its dismal length could boast but one of those substantial old red-brick mansions whose occasional appearance redeemed the commonness of the other high roads. There was a sprinkling of humble shops, a seamen's lodging-house, a terrace or two of shabby-genteel houses, three-storied, with little iron balconies that had never been painted within the memory of man; poor sordid-looking little houses, which were always putting bills in their smoke-darkened windows, beseeching people to come and lodge in them. There were a few modern villas, of the speculative-builders' pattern, whose smart freshness put to shame their surroundings; and one of these, a corner one, with about half a perch of garden-ground, was distinguished by a red lamp and a brass-plate, on which appeared the following inscription:

Mr. Lucius Davoren,
Surgeon.

Here Lucius Davoren had begun the battle of life; actual life, in all its cold reality; hard and common and monotonous, and on occasion hopeless; a life strangely different from the explorer's adventurous days, from the trapper's lonely commune with nature in the trackless pine-woods; a life wherein the veriest dreamer could find scant margin for poetry; a life whose dull realities weigh down the soul of man as though an iron hand were laid upon his brain, grinding out every aspiration for better things than the day's food and the night's shelter.

He stands alone in the world; there is comfort at least in that. Let the struggle be sharp as it may, there is no cherished companion to share the pain. Let poverty's stern grip pinch him never so sharply, he feels the pinch alone. Father, mother, the child sister, whom he loved so dearly fifteen years ago, are all dead. Their graves lie far away in a Hampshire churchyard, the burial-place of that rural village of which his father was Rector for thirty years of his unambitious life.

He has another sister, but she was counted lost some years ago, and to think of her is worse than to think of the dead. In all those years, from the time when he was a lad just emancipated from Winchester school to this present hour, he has never been heard to speak her name; but he keeps her in his memory nevertheless, and has the record of her hapless fate hidden away in the secret-drawer of his desk, with a picture of the face whose beauty was fatal.

She was his favourite sister, his senior by two years, fond and proud of him, his counsellor and ally in all things; like himself, passionately fond of music; like himself a born musician. This charm, in conjunction with her beauty, had made her the glory and **delight** of a small provincial circle, which widened before her influence. Wykhamston society was **the** narrowest and stiffest of systems; but the **fame** of Janet Davoren's beauty and Janet Davoren's voice travelled beyond **the** bounds of Wykhamston society. In a word, Miss Davoren was taken notice of by the county. The **meek** old Rector, with his pleasant face, and bald head scantily garnished with iron-gray hair, was made to emerge from retirement, in order **to** gratify the county. He was bidden to a ball **at** the Marquis of Guildford's; to a private concert at Sir Horatio and Lady Veering Baker's; **to** dinners and evening parties twenty miles away from the modest Rectory. Miss Davoren was even invited to stay at Lady Baker's; and, going ostensibly for a few days, remained her ladyship's guest for nearly a month. They were all so fond of the dear girl, Lady Baker informed the Rector.

'*I* am not **good enough**, I suppose,' said Mrs. Davoren, when the Marchioness and the Baronet's wife, after calling upon her, and being intensely civil for fifteen minutes, ignored her in their cards of invitation. 'Never mind, Stephen, if you **and Janet** enjoy yourselves, I'm satisfied; and it's lucky they haven't invited me, for I've nothing to wear but my old black satin and the Indian scarf, and *they*'d never do for the Castle or Lady Veering Baker's. They're well enough in Wykhamston, where people are accustomed to them.'

So the Rector's worthy wife, who had supreme control of the family purse, arrayed her handsome daughter in the prettiest dresses the Wykhamston milliner could achieve, and ornamented the girl's dark hair with camelias from the little green-house, and was content to sit at home and wonder what the grand Castle folks thought of her Janet, and whether her dear old man was having an agreeable rubber; content to sit up late into the night, while the rectory handmaidens snored in their attic chambers, till the creaky old covered wagonette brought home the revellers, when she would sit up yet another hour to hear the tidings of her darling's triumphs; what songs she had sung, what dances she had danced, and all the gracious things that had been said of her and to her.

About this time, the idea that Miss Davoren was destined to make a splendid marriage became a fixed belief in the minds of the Rector's family, from the head thereof to the very cook who cooked the dinner, always excepting the young lady herself, who seemed to take very little thought of anything but music; the organ which she played in the old church; the old-fashioned square piano in the rectory drawing-room. It did not seem possible to the simple mind of Mrs. Davoren that all this admiration could result in nothing; that her daughter could be the cynosure of every eye at Guildford Castle, the acknowledged belle at Lady Veering Baker's musical evenings, and yet remain plain Janet Davoren, or be reduced to the necessity of marrying a curate or a struggling country surgeon. Something must come of all this patronage, which had kindled the fire of jealousy in many a Wykhamston breast. But when the fond mother ventured to suggest as much to the girl herself, she was put off with affectionate reproof.

'Dearest mother, can you be so innocent as not to see that all this notice means nothing more than the gratification of the moment? The Marchioness and Lady Baker had happened to hear that I sing tolerably, and as the common run of amateur music is not worth much, thought they might as well have me. It only cost the trouble of calling upon you, and pretending to be interested in your poultry and papa's garden. If this were London, and they could get professional singers, they would not have taken even so much trouble as that about me.'

'Never mind what the Marchioness and Lady Baker mean,' said the mother; 'I am not thinking of them, but of the people you meet there; the young men who pay you such compliments, and crowd round you after your songs.'

Janet laughed, almost bitterly, at this speech and at the mother's eager look, full of anticipated triumph.

'And who will go back to their own world and forget my existence, when they leave Hampshire,' she said.

'But there must be some whose attentions are more marked than others,' urged Mrs. Davoren; 'county people, perhaps. There is that Mr. Cumbermere, for instance, who has an immense estate on the borders of Berkshire. I've heard your papa talk of him; quite a young man, and unmarried. Come, Janet, be candid with your poor old mother. Isn't there one among them all who seems a little in earnest?'

'Not one among them, mother,' the girl answered, looking downward with a faint, faint sigh, so faint as to escape even the mother's ear; 'not one. They all say the same thing, or the same kind of thing, in just the same way. They think me rather good-looking, I believe, and they seem really to like my singing and playing. But they will go away and forget both, and my good looks as well. There is not one of them ever so little in love with me; and if I were in love with **one of them** I might almost **as well be** in love with all, for they are all alike.'

This was discouraging, but the mother still cherished her dream; cherished it until the bitter hour of awakening—that fatal hour in which she learned from a letter in the girl's own hand **that** Janet had abandoned home, **friends,** reputation—the very hope of heaven, as it seemed to the heartbroken father and mother—to follow the fortunes of a villain, of whose identity they had not the faintest idea, whose opportunities for the compassing of this deadly work would seem to have been of the smallest.

The girl's letter—passionate, despairing, **with a** wild and deep despair which told how desperate had been the conflict between love and duty—gave no hint of her betrayer's name or place in the world.

The letter was somewhat vaguely worded. There are some things which no woman could **write.** Janet Davoren did not tell them **that** she went of her own free will to perdition. But so much despair could hardly accompany an innocent passion; sorrow so deep and hopeless implied guilt. To the Rector and his wife there seemed no room for doubt. They read and re-read the long wild appeal for forgiveness or oblivion; **that** their **only** daughter, the pride and idol of both, might be pardoned or forgotten. They weighed every word, written with a swift impetuous hand, blotted by remorseful tears, but no ray of hope shone between the lines. They could arrive at but one miserable conclusion. The girl had accepted dishonour as the cost of a love she was too weak to renounce. The letter was long, wild, recklessly worded; but in all there was no clue to the traitor.

The Rector and his wife made no outcry. They were even heroic enough to suppress all outward token of their grief, lest their little world should discover the cruel truth. The father went about his daily work pale and shaken, but calm of aspect. The only noticeable fact in his life was that from this day forth he neglected his garden and his poultry-yard. His innocent delight in Dorking fowls and standard rose-trees perished for ever with his daughter's disappearance. The mother wept in secret, and suffered not so much as a single tear to be seen by her household.

The servants were told that Miss Davoren had gone upon a visit to some friends in London. Janet had left the house in the early morning, unseen by any one except the lad who attended to the garden, and him she had employed to convey a small portmanteau to the railway station. The manner of her departure therefore had been commonplace enough; but the servants were accustomed to hear a good deal of preliminary discussion before any movement of the family, and wondered not a little that there should have been nothing said about Miss Davoren's departure beforehand, and that she should have gone away so early, before any one was up, and without so much as a cup of tea, as the cook remarked plaintively.

The wretched father and mother read that farewell letter till every word it contained seemed written on their hearts, but it helped them in no manner towards the knowledge of their daughter's fate. They went over the names in their own little circle; the half-dozen or so of young men—more or less unattractive—who were on visiting terms at the Rectory; but there was no member of Wykhamston society they could for a moment consider guilty; and indeed, the answer to every suspicion was obvious in the fact that every member of that small community was in his place: the curate going his quiet rounds on a hog-maned pony; the unmarried doctor scouring the neighbourhood from breakfast to tea-time in his travel-worn dog-cart; the lawyer's son true to the articles that bound him to his father's service; the small landowners and gentlemanly tenant-farmers of the immediate vicinity to be seen as of old at church and market-place. No, there was no one the Rector could suspect of act or part in his darling's flight.

A little later, and with extreme caution, he ventured to inquire among certain of his parishioners if any stranger had been seen about Wykhamston within the last month or so. He contrived to put this question to a well-to-do corn-chandler, the chief gossip of the little town, in a purely conversational manner.

'Yes,' said Mr. Huskings the corn-chandler, assenting to a general remark upon the dulness that had prevailed of late in Wykhamston, 'the place has been quiet enough. It ain't much of a place for strangers at the best of times, unless it's one of them measuring chaps that come spying about, with a yard measure, after a new railway, that's to take everybody away from the town and never bring nobody to it, and raise the price of meat and vegibles. There was that horgan-playin' chap at the George the other day; what *he* come for nobody could find out, for he didn't measure nothing; only poked about the old church on workadays, and played the horgan. But of course you'd know all about him from Miss Davoren, as must have seen him sometimes when she went to practise with the coheer.'

The Rector's sad face blanched a little. This was the man!

'No,' he said, somewhat falteringly, 'my daughter never spoke of him; or if she did I didn't take any notice. She's away now for a little time, staying with friends in London. She may have told us about him; I don't remember.'

'Strange old gentleman, the Rector!' Mr. Huskings remarked to his wife afterwards; 'such a nervous way with him lately; breaking fast, I'm afeard.'

'Miss Davoren could hardly have missed seein' of him,' he answered. 'He were always about the church, when he warn't fishin', but he were a great hand at fishin'. Rather a well-looking chap, with dark eyes and long dark hair; looked summat like a furriner, but spoke English plain enough in spite of his furrin looks.'

'Young?' asked the Rector.

'Might be anything betwixt twenty-five and thirty-five.'

'And a gentleman, I suppose?'

'His clothes was fust-class, and he paid his way honourable. Had the best rooms over yonder,' with a jerk of his head in the direction of the George, 'and tipped everybody 'andsome. He warn't here above a month or six weeks; but he hired a pianner from Mr. Stammers, up street, and there he'd sit by the hour together, Mrs. Capon told me, strum, strum, strum. "Music that made you feel creepy-crawly like," says Mrs. Capon; "not a good hearty tune as you could understand, but meandering and meandering like till you felt as if you'd gone to sleep in a cathedral while the organ was playin'," says Mrs. Capon.'

Music! Yes, that was the spell which had lured his child to her ruin. Nothing less than that fatal magic, which had held her from her babyhood, could have been strong enough to beguile that poor young soul.

'Did you hear the man's name?' asked the Rector.

'I heerd it, sure enough, sir; but I never were a good hand at remembering names. Mrs. Capon ud tell you in a moment.'

'No, no,' exclaimed the Rector nervously; 'I've no curiosity; it's of no importance. Good-afternoon, Huskings. You—you may send me a sack of barley;' this with a little pang, remembering what a joyless business his poultry-yard had become of late.

He went 'up street' to Mr. Stammers, who kept a little music-shop and let out pianos.

'You'd better look in at the Rectory and tune the

piano before my daughter comes home, Stammers,' said the Rector, with a bitter pain at his heart, and then sat down in the chair by Mr. Stammers' door—set wide open on this warm afternoon—a little out of breath, though the High-street from the corn-merchant's door to the music-seller's was a dead level.

'Yes, sir. Miss Davoren away, sir? I thought I missed her at church last Sunday. Mr. Filby's playing don't come anything nigh hers. What a wonderful gift she has, sir! The Marchioness was up town yesterday—they are at the Castle for a week, ong parsong—and drew up here to give an order. I made bold to show her the little fantasia I took the liberty to dedicate to Miss Davoren. She smiled so sweet when she saw the name. "You've reason to be proud of your Rector's daughter, Mr. Stammers," she said; "such a lovely young lady, and such a fine musician! I wish I had time to call at the Rectory." And then she arst after your 'elth, sir, and your good lady's, and Miss Davoren's, quite affable, just before she drove away. She was drivin' her own ponies.'

'She was very good,' said Mr. Davoren absently. O, vain delight in earthly pomp and pride! The notice of these magnates of the land had not saved his child from destruction; nay, perhaps had been, in some unknown manner, the primary cause of her fall.

'Yes, you had better tune the piano, Stammers,' he went on, with a feeble sigh. 'She will like to find it in good tune when she comes back. By the way, you let a piano to the gentleman at the George the other day—Mr.—'

'Mr. Vandeleur,' said Stammers briskly. 'Let him the best piano I have—a brand-new Collard— at thirty shillings a month, bein', as it was, a short let. And wonderful it was to hear him play upon it, too! I've stood on the staircase at the George half an hour at a stretch, listenin' to him.'

'A fine musician?' inquired the Rector, with another sigh. Fatal music, deadly art!

'Fine isn't the word, sir. There's a many fine musicians, as far as pianoforte playing goes,' with a little conscious air of inward swelling, as of a man who numbered himself among these gifted ones. 'I don't think there's anythink of Mozart's, or 'Andel's, or 'Aydn's, or Beethoven's—that's the king of 'em all, is Beethoven—you could put a name to that I wouldn't play at sight; but I don't rank myself with Mr. Vandeleur, the gentleman at the George, for all that.'

'What is the difference?'

Mr. Stammers tapped his forehead.

'There, sir; there's where the difference lies. I 'aven't 'is 'ead. Not but what I had a taste for music when I was that 'igh,' indicating the altitude of a foot and a half from the floor, 'and was took notice of by the gentry of these parts in consequence, my father bein', as you are aware, sir, a numble carpenter. But I 'aven't the 'ead that man 'as. To hear him 'andle Beethoven, sir, the Sonater Pathetick, or the "Moonlight," wonderful! And not that alone. There was sonaters and fugues he played, sir—whether they was his own composition or wasn't, I can't say; but they were fugues and sonaters I never heard before, and I don't believe mortal man ever wrote 'em. They outraged all the laws of 'armony, sir. Why, there was consecutive fifths in 'em as thick as gooseberries, and yet they was as fine as anythink in Mozart. Such music! It turned one's blood cold to hear him. If you could fancy the old gentleman playing the piano—which, bein' a clergyman, of course you wouldn't give your mind to—you could fancy him playing like that.'

'An eccentric style?' inquired the Rector.

'Eccentric! It was the topsy-turviest kind of thing I ever heard in my life. Yet if that man was to play in public, he'd take the town by storm; they'd run after him like mad.'

'Do you think he is a professional performer?'

'Hardly; he hadn't the professional way with him. I've seen plenty of the profession, havin' managed for all the concerts that have been given in Wykhamston for the last twenty years. No; and a professional wouldn't dawdle away close upon six weeks in a small country town such as this. No; what I take him for is a wealthy amateur—a gentleman that had been living a little too fast up in London, and come down here to freshen himself up a bit with country air and quiet.'

'How did he spend his time?'

'In the church, a good bit of it, playing the organ. He used to get the keys from old Bopolt, the clerk. I wonder you didn't hear of it, sir.'

'No,' said the Rector, 'they told me nothing.' This with a sigh so deep, so near akin to a groan, that it smote the heart of the lively Stammers.

'I'm afraid you're tired, sir, this 'ot day—tryin' weather—so changeable; the thermumitor has gone up to eighty-one, Farren's heat. Can I get you a glass of water, sir, with a dash of somethink, if I might take the liberty?'

'Thank you, Stammers; no, it's nothing. I've

been a little worried lately. Bopolt had no business to admit any one into the church habitually.'

'I daresay Mr. Vandeleur made it worth his while, sir. He was quite a gentleman, I assure you. And it wasn't as if you was in the 'abit of keepin' the sacramential plate in the vestry.'

'There are other things that a man can steal,' said the Rector moodily; 'more precious things than paten or chalice. But no matter. I don't suppose Bopolt meant any harm, only—only he might have told me. Good-afternoon, Mr. Stammers.'

'Do you feel yourself strong enough for the walk 'ome, sir? You look rather pale—overcome by the 'eat.'

'Yes, yes; quite strong. Good-afternoon;' and Stephen Davoren plodded his way down the shadeless High-street till he came to a little court leading to the church; Wykhamston Church being, for some reason or other, hidden away at the back of the High-street, as though it were an unsightly thing, and only approachable by courts and alleys.

Old John Bopolt, the parish clerk, quavering and decrepit after the manner of rural clerks, had his habitation in the court which made the isthmus of communication between the High-street and the churchyard. He rose hastily from his tea-table at sight of his Rector, and made a little old-world bow, while Mrs. Bopolt and Mrs. Bopolt's married daughter, and the married daughter's Betsy Jane, an unkempt girl of fourteen or so, huddled together with a respectful and awestricken air before that dignitary.

'Bopolt,' said the Rector, in a sterner tone than he was wont to use, 'what right had you to allow the church to be made a lounging-place for idle strangers?'

'A lounging-place, sir! I never did any suchlike thing. There was no lounging went on, to my knowledge; but I've been in the habit of showing the monniments occasionally, as you know, sir, to any respectable stranger, and the rose winder over the south door.'

'Showing the monuments; yes, that's one thing. But to let a stranger have the key habitually—'

'Meanin' the gentleman at the George, sir,' faltered the clerk, with an embarrassed air. 'He was quite the gentleman; and Mr. Filby, the organist, sir, knew as he was in the 'abit of playin' the organ for a 'our or so, and left the keys for him regular, did Mr. Filby, and says to me, "John, whenever Mr. Vandeleur at the George likes to play the organ, he's free and welcome, and you can tell him so, with my respects."'

'He bribed you, I suppose?' said Mr. Davoren.

'He may have given me a trifle at odd times as some recompensation for my trouble in opening the door for him, sir. I don't wish to deceive you; and if I'd thought for a moment there was any harm, I'd have cut my fingers off sooner than open the church-door for him. But I made certain as you knew, sir, more particularly as I'd seen Miss Davoren go into the church more than once when Mr. Vandeleur was there.'

'Of course,' said the Rector, without flinching, 'she had her choir work to attend to. Well, John, there's no use in being angry about a mistake; only remember the church is not a place for the amusement of amateur musicians. Good-afternoon.'

The family, who had looked on in unspeakable awe during this brief dialogue, now began to breathe freely again, and a kettle, which had been sputtering destruction over Mrs. Bopolt's bright fender unregarded, was now snatched off the top bar by that careful matron, who had not dared to move hand or foot in the presence of an offended Rector.

Stephen Davoren walked slowly homeward, a little more sick at heart than when he began his voyage of discovery. Other people had known the seducer; other people had seen his daughter go into the church to meet her tempter, polluting that sacred place by the conflict of an earthly passion. Other people had guessed something of the dreadful truth, perhaps. He only had been blind.

The thought of this, that his little world might be in the secret of his sad story, helped to break his heart. If it had not been broken by the mere fact of his daughter's ruin, it would have been crushed by the weight of his own shame. He could not look the world in the face any more. He tried to do his duty manfully, preached the old sound homely sermons; but when he spoke of sin and sorrow, he seemed to speak of his lost daughter. He went among his poor, but the thought of Janet set his wits wandering in the midst of his simple talk, and he would make little feeble speeches, and repeat himself helplessly, hardly knowing what he said.

His parishioners perceived the change, and told each other that the Rector was breaking fast; it was a pity Miss Davoren was away: 'She'd have cheered him up a bit, poor old gentleman.'

Lucius came home from Winchester later in the year—his school course ended, and the winner of a scholarship which would help him at the university —came home to hear the story of his sister's flight, his Janet, the sister whose genius and beauty had been his highest pride.

He took the news of this calamity more quietly than his father and mother had dared to hope; insisted upon hearing every detail of the event, but said little.

'You made inquiries about this man, this Mr. Vandeleur, of course, father?' he said.

'Yes,' answered the Rector in his despondent way, 'I wrote to Harwood—you remember my old friend Harwood, the solicitor?—and set him to work, not telling him the whole story, as you may suppose. But it resulted in nothing. I put an advertisement into the *Times*, too, imploring your sister—' with a little husky noise before the word, as if he would fain have uttered his missing girl's name but could not, 'imploring her to come back, offering forgiveness, affection, silence, so worded that none but she could understand. I think she must have left England, Lucius. I do not believe she would have left that appeal unanswered.'

'Vandeleur!' said Lucius quietly; 'an assumed name, no doubt. Some scoundrel she met at the Castle, or at Lady Baker's. Vandeleur, I pray God I may come across him before I'm many years older.'

This was all he said, and from this time forth he never pronounced his sister's name. He saw how far this grief had gone towards shortening his father's life, how dark a cloud it had spread over his mother's declining years. A twelvemonth later, and both were gone; the father dying suddenly one bright spring morning of heart-disease, organic disorder of long standing, but who shall say how accelerated by that bitter trouble? The faithful wife drooped from the day of her husband's death, and only four months afterwards sank quietly to her rest, thankful that her journey was ended, placidly happy in the secure hope of a swift and easy passage to the better land, where she would find the partner of her life waiting for her, the little daughter who died years ago greeting her with loving welcome.

And thus Lucius Davoren had been left quite alone in the world in the first year of his university life, two years before he came up to London to walk the hospitals, and just five years before he started for America with Geoffrey Hossack.

CHAPTER II.

HOMER SIVEWRIGHT.

There was not a plethora of patients in the Shadrack-road, nor were the cases which presented themselves to Mr. Davoren for the most part of a deeply-interesting character. He had a good supply of casualties, from broken limbs, dislocated shoulders, collar bones, and crushed ribs, down to black eyes; he had numerous cases of a purely domestic nature —cases which called him out of his bed of nights; and he had a good many small patients in the narrow streets and airless alleys—little sufferers whose quiet endurance, whose meek acceptance of pain as a necessity of their lives, moved him more than he would have cared to confess. So profound a pity as he sometimes felt for these little ones would have seemed hardly professional. His practice among children was singularly fortunate. He did not drench them with those nauseous compounds which previous practitioners had freely administered in a rough-and-ready off-hand fashion; but he did, with a very small amount of drugs, for the most part succeed in setting these delicate machines in order, restoring health's natural hue to pallid cheeks, breathing life into feeble lungs. It was painful to him often to find himself obliged to prescribe good broths and nourishing solids where an empty larder and an unfurnished purse stared him, as it were, palpably in the face; and there were many occasions when he eked out his instructions with contributions in kind — a shilling's worth of beef or a couple of mutton-chops, from the butcher at the end of the street, a gill of port from the nearest tavern. But him, too, Poverty held in his iron grip, and it was not always that he could afford to part with so much as a shilling.

Such luxuries as fresh air and clean water— restoratives which might be supposed easy of access even in the Shadrack-road district, though there were dwellings around and about Shadrack Basin where even these were hardly obtainable—he urged upon his patients with all his might, and in the households he attended there arose a startling innovation in the way of open windows. From these very poor patients he, of course, received no money; but he had other patrons, small tradesmen and their families, who paid him, and paid him honourably, down on the nail for the most part, and on a scale he felt he must blush to remember by and by when he became a distinguished west-end physician. Small as the payments were, however, they enabled him to live, so very small were his own requirements. His Amati ate nothing. He had, himself, a stoical indifference to good living, and could have sustained himself contentedly upon pemmican, within reach of all the richest and rarest viands earth could yield to a Lucullus. His establishment consisted of an ancient serving-woman, who had withdrawn herself from a useful career of charing for his exclusive service, a woman who returned to the bosom of her family every night and came back to her post in the early morning, and a boy of a low-spirited turn of mind and an inconvenient tendency to bleeding at the nose. It irked him that he was obliged to pay the rent of an entire house, however small, requiring for his own uses at most three rooms. But people had told him that he could not hope to do any good in the Shadrack-Basin district if he began his professional career in lodgings; and he was fain to submit. He concluded that there must be some lurking element of aristocracy in the minds of the

Shadrackites, not suggested by their outward habits, which were of the whelk-and-periwinkle-eating order.

His house was small, inconvenient, and shabbily furnished. He had taken the furniture at a valuation from Mr. Plumsole, his predecessor — a valuation which, if it had been based on justice, should have been nothing; since a more rickety race of chairs and tables, a more evil-looking family of bedsteads and dressing-tables, chiffoniers and sofas, had never been called into being by the glue-pot. There was not a perfect set of castors in the house, or a chair which had not some radical defect in one of its legs, or a table that realised one's notion of a correct level. Lucius was obliged to buy a tool-box and a glue-pot very soon after his investiture as proprietor of Mr. Plumsole's goods and chattels; and a good deal of his leisure was consumed by small experiments in domestic surgery, as applied to chairs and tables. He performed the most delicate operations; reduced dislocations, and cured compound fractures in a wonderful way; with the aid of a handful of tin tacks and a halfpennyworth of glue. But he felt somehow that this was not the direct road to the mastery of a great science, and would give a weary little sigh as he went back to his medical books, after a sharp struggle with a refractory chair-leg, or an obstinate declivity in the flap of a Pembroke table.

He was very poor, very patient, very much in earnest; as earnest now as he had been in those days of wild adventure in the Far West, when amid all the excitement of the chase his thoughts had ever gone beyond, searching for Nature's secrets, longing to wrest from her vast stores of hidden wealth some treasure which might be useful to his fellow-creatures. Of all those vague unspoken hopes nothing had come. He had left no footmark behind him in that distant world; he had brought home no trophy. Nothing had resulted from all those days of hardship and peril, except a secret which it was horror to remember. He turned his face now resolutely to the real world—the cold, hard, workaday world of an over-populated city—and set himself to do what good there was for him to do in his narrow sphere.

'It may be some atonement for the blood I shed yonder,' he said to himself.

In his small way he prospered—prospered in doing good. When he had been at this drudgery a little more than a year, the parish surgeon died— popular report said of a too genial temper and a leaning towards good fellowship, not unassociated with Irish whisky—and Lucius was elected in his stead.

This gave him a pittance which helped him, paid his rent and taxes and the charwoman, and gave him admittance to the dwellings of the poor. Thus it was he came to have so many children in his case-book, and to spend his scanty surplus in small charities among his patients.

He worked hard all day, and, after the manner of his kind, was often called up in the night; but he had his evenings for the most part to himself, to use as he listed. These precious intervals of leisure he spent in reading—reading which was chiefly professional—solacing himself sometimes with a dip into a favourite author. His library consisted of a shelf-full of books on one of the decrepit chiffoniers, and was at least select. The Greek playwrights, Shakespeare, Montaigne, St. Thomas à Kempis, Molière, Sterne, De Musset, Shelley, Keats, Byron made up his stock; and of these he never knew weariness. He opened one of these volumes haphazard when the scientific reading had been unusually tough, and he had closed his medical books with a sigh of relief, opened one of his pet volumes anywhere, and read on till he read himself into dreamland. Dreams will come, even in the Shadrack-Basin district, to a man who has not yet crossed the boundary line of his thirtieth birthday; but Lucius Davoren's were only vague dreams, inchoate visions of future success, of the days when he was to be famous, and live among the lofty spirits of the age, and feel that he had made his name a name to be remembered in centuries to come. Perhaps every young man who has been successful at a public school and at the university begins life with the same vision; but upon Lucius the fancy had a stronger hold than on most men, and almost amounted to a belief, the belief that it was his destiny to be of use to his fellow-creatures.

But he had another key to open the gates of dreamland, a key more potent than Shakespeare. When things had gone well with him, when in the day's work there had been some little professional success, some question that interested his keen fancy, and had been solved to his satisfaction; above all, when he had done some good thing for his fellow-creatures, he would take a shining mahogany-case from the chiffonier beneath his book-shelf, lay it tenderly on the table, as if it were a living thing, open it with a dainty little key which he wore attached to his watch-chain, and draw forth his priceless treasure, the Amati violin, for which he, to whom pounds were verily pounds, had given in his early student days the sum of one hundred guineas. How many deprivations, how many small sacrifices—gloves, opera-tickets, ay, even dinners—that violin represented! He naturally loved it so much the better for the pangs it had cost him. He had earned it, if not with the sweat of his brow, at least by the exercise of supreme self-denial.

Then, with careful hand, with delicate sympathetic touch, fingers light as those with which a woman gathers her favourite flower, he would draw forth his fiddle, and soon the little room would be filled with gentle strains—plaintive, soothing, meditative, the music of dreams; full of tender thoughts, of pensive memories; music which was like thinking aloud. And after those fond memories of familiar melody, music which was as easy a language as his mother tongue, he would open one of his battered old volumes, and pore over the intricate pages of Viotti, or Spohr, or De Beriot, or Lafont, until midnight, and even the quieter hours that follow, had sounded from all the various steeple-clocks and dockyard-clocks and factory-clocks of that watery district.

He had been working upwards of a year as parish surgeon, and in all that time, and the time that went before it, had not been favoured with any more aristocratic patronage than that of the neighbouring tradesmen, his wealthiest patient being a publican at the corner of the great Essex-road, reported the richest man in the district; when chance, or that combination of small causes which seems generally to lead up to the greatest effects, brought him into friendly and professional relations with a man of a different class; a man about whom the Shadrack-road knew little, but thought much.

Lucius was returning from his daily round one winter afternoon, towards the end of November, when the skies that roof in the Shadrack-Basin region begin to darken soon after three o'clock. It was nearer five when the parish surgeon set his face homeward, and the Shadrack-road was enfolded in its customary fog; the street-lamps—not too brilliant in the clearest weather—and the lighted shop-windows showing dimly athwart that sombre smoke-curtain. Suddenly, gleaming a little brighter than the rest, he saw a moving lamp, the lamp of a fast hansom; then heard an execration, in the usual cab-man-voice; a crash, a grinding noise as of wheels grating against wheels; a volley of execrations rising in terrible crescendo; and then the loud commanding voice of the passenger in the stranded vehicle, demanding to be let out.

Lucius went to the assistance of the distressed passenger—if that could be called distress which could command so lusty an utterance — and extricated him from the hansom, which had run foul of a monster dray, laden with beer barrels.

The passenger availed himself of Mr. Davoren's arm, and alighted, not without some show of feebleness. It seemed as if his chief strength were in his voice. Seen somewhat dimly beneath that fog curtain, he appeared an old man, tall but bent, with a leonine head and a penetrating eye—keen as the eye of hawk or eagle.

He thanked the surgeon briefly, dismissed the cabman with a stern reproof and without his fare.

'You know me,' he said; 'Homer Sivewright, Cedar House. You can take out a summons if you fancy you're badly treated. You've jerked a great deal more than eighteenpence out of my constitution.'

The cabman vanished in the fog, grumbling but acquiescent.

'At seventy and upwards,' said Mr. Sivewright to Lucius, 'the human economy will hardly bear shaking. I shall walk home.'

He seemed feeble, somewhat uncertain upon his legs; and Lucius's humanity came to the rescue.

'Take my arm as far as your house,' he said ' my time is not especially valuable.'

'Isn't it?' demanded the old man, looking at him suspiciously; 'a young man about London whose time is of no use to him is in a bad road.'

'I didn't say my time was of no use to me. Perhaps there are not many men in London who work harder than I. Only, as I take no pleasure, I have sometimes a margin left after work. I can spare half-an-hour just now, and if you like to lean on my arm it is at your service.'

'I accept your friendly offer. You speak like a gentleman and an honest man. My house is not half a mile from here; you must know it if you know this neighbourhood—Cedar House.'

'I think I do. A curious old house, belonging evidently to two periods, half stone, half brick, standing back from the road behind a heavily-buttressed wall. Is that it?'

'Yes. It was once a palace or a royal hunting-lodge, or whatever you like to call it. It was afterwards enlarged, in the reign of Anne, and became a wealthy citizen's country seat, before there were all these abominations of factories and ropewalks and docks between the City and the eastern suburbs. I got the place for an almost nominal rent, and it suits me, as an empty hogshead would suit a mouse —plenty of room to turn round in it.'

'The house looks very large, but your family is large, no doubt.'

'My family consists of myself and my granddaughter, with two old servants,— trustworthy, of course. That is to say, they have learned by experience exactly to what extent they may safely rob me.'

They were walking in an eastward direction as they talked; the old man leaning somewhat heavily on the younger.

Lucius laughed pleasantly at his companion's cynicism.

'Then you don't believe even in the honesty of faithful servants?'

'I believe in nothing that is not demonstrable by the rule of three. The fidelity of old servants is like the fidelity of your household cat—they are faithful to their places; the beds they have slept upon so many years; the fireside at which they have a snug corner where the east wind cannot touch their rheumatism.'

'Yet there are instances of something better than mere feline constancy. Sir Walter Scott's servants, for instance, who put their shoulders to the wheel manfully when Fortune played their master false— the old butler turning scrub and jack-of-all-trades, the old coachman going to the plough-tail. There is something awful in the descent of a butler, too, like the downfall of an archbishop.'

'I don't know anything about your Sir Walter Scott,' growled Mr. Sivewright; 'I suppose it is natural to youth to look at all things brightly, though I have known youth that didn't. You talk gaily enough for a young man who devotes no time to pleasure.'

'Do you think pleasure—in the common acceptation of the word, meaning late hours and mixed company—really conduces to good spirits?'

'Only as opium engenders sleep—to leave a man three times as wakeful afterwards,' said Mr. Sivewright. 'I have done without that kind of pleasure myself throughout a long life, yet I hardly count myself wise. Fairly to estimate the lightness of his own particular burden, a man should try to carry a heavier one. There is no better tonic for the hard-worker than a course of pleasure. You are in some trade or profession, I presume,' he added, turning his sharp glance upon his companion; 'a clerk, perhaps?'

'No; but something that works harder than a clerk. A parish doctor.'

Mr. Sivewright recoiled palpably.

'Don't be alarmed,' said Lucius; 'it was not as a possible patient that I pulled you out of the cab. My practice doesn't lie among the upper classes.'

'Nor do I belong to the upper classes,' answered the other quickly. 'I forgive you your profession, though I am among those prejudiced people who have an innate aversion from doctors, lawyers, and parsons. But the machinery of commerce won't allow us to dispense with the lawyers; and I suppose among the poor there still lingers a remnant of the old belief that there's some use in doctors. The parsons thrive upon the foolishness of women. So there is a field still left for your three learned professions.'

'That way of talking is a fashion,' said Lucius quietly; 'but I daresay if you were seriously ill tomorrow, your thoughts would turn instinctively towards Savile-row. And perhaps if you were going to die, you'd feel all the happier if the friendly voice of your parish priest breathed familiar words of hope and comfort beside your pillow.'

'I know nothing of my parish, except that its rates are four-and-twopence in the pound,' returned the other in his incisive voice.

A quarter of an hour's walking, beguiled by such talk as this, brought them to the house of which Lucius had spoken, a dwelling altogether out of keeping with the present character of the Shadrack-road. That heavily-buttressed wall, dark with the smoke and foul weather of centuries; that rusty iron gate, with its florid scroll work, and forgotten coat-of-arms (a triumph of the blacksmith's art two hundred years old); that dark-browed building within, formed of a red-brick centre, square, many-windowed, and prosaic, with a tall narrow doorway, overshadowed by a stone shell, sustained by cherubic heads of the Anne period, flanked by an older wing of gray moss-discoloured stone, with massive mullioned windows, had nothing in common with the shabby rows and shops and skimpy terraces and bulkheads and low-roofed, disreputable habitations of the neighbourhood. It stood alone, a solitary relic of the past; splendid, gloomy, inscrutable.

Nothing in the man Sivewright interested Lucius Davoren half so much as the fact that he lived in this queer old house. After all a man's surroundings are often half the man, and our first impression of a new acquaintance is generally taken from his chairs and tables.

The grim old iron gate was not a portal to be opened with a latch-key. It looked like one of the outworks of a fortification, to be taken by assault. Mr. Sivewright pulled at an iron ring, suspended beyond the reach of the gutter children of the district, and a remote bell rang within the fastness, a hoarse old bell, rusty no doubt like the gate. After a lengthy interval measured by the gauge of a visitor's patience, but which Mr. Sivewright accepted with resignation as a thing of course, this summons produced an elderly female, with slippered feet, a bonnet, and bare arms, who unlocked the gate, and admitted them to an enclosure of fog, stagnant as compared with the fog in circulation without, and which seemed to the doctor of a lower temperature, as if in crossing that narrow boundary he had travelled a degree northward.

'Come in,' said Mr. Sivewright, with the tone of a man who offers reluctant hospitality, 'and have a glass of wine. You've had a cold walk on my account; you'd better take a little refreshment.'

'No, thanks; but I should like to see your house.'

'Should you? There's not much to see; an old barrack, that's all,' said the old man, stopping short, with a doubtful air, as if he would have infinitely preferred leaving the surgeon outside. 'Very few strangers ever cross my threshold, except the tax-gatherer. However,' with an air of resignation, 'come in.'

The old woman had opened the tall narrow door

meanwhile, revealing an interior dimly lighted by a lamp which must have been feeble always, but which was now the veriest glimmer. Lucius followed his new acquaintance through this doorway into a large square hall, from which a broad oaken staircase ascended to an open gallery. There was just enough light for Lucius to see that this hall, instead of being bare and meagrely furnished as he had expected to find it, was crowded with a vast assemblage of heterogeneous objects. Pictures piled against the gloomy panelled walls. Sculpture, porcelain, and delf of every nation and every period, from monster vases of imperial lacquer to fragile déjeuners of Dresden and Copenhagen; from inchoate groups of vermin and shell-fish from the workshop of Pallissy, to the exquisite modelling of teacups resplendent with gods and goddesses from Capo-di-Monte; from gaudy dishes and bowls of old Rouen delf, to the perfection of Louis-Seize Sèvres. Armour of every age, vases of jasper and porphyry, carved-oak cabinets, the particoloured plumage of stuffed birds, Gobelins tapestry, South-Sea shells, Venetian glass, Milan ironwork, were curiously intermingled; as if some maniac artist in the confusion of a once fine taste had heaped these things together. By that dim light, Lucius saw only the fitful glimmer of steel casques and breastplates, the half-defined shapes of marble statues, the outline of jasper vases and huge Pallissy dishes. Later he came to know all those treasures by heart.

A Louis-Quatorze clock on a bracket began to strike six, and immediately a chorus of clocks in adjacent rooms, in tones feeble or strong, tenor or bass, took up the strain.

'I am like Charles the Fifth, particular about my clocks,' said Mr. Sivewright. 'I keep them all going. This way, if you please, Mr.—'

'Davoren.'

'Davoren! That sounds a good name.'

'My father cherished a tradition to that effect—a good middle-class family. Our ancestor represented his native county in Queen Elizabeth's first Parliament. But I inherited nothing except the name.'

He was staring about him in that doubtful light, as he spoke, trying to penetrate the gloom.

'You are surprised to see such a collection as that in the Shadrack-road? Dismiss your wonder. I am not an antiquarian; but a dealer. Those things represent the remnant of my stock-in-trade. I kept a shop in Bond-street for five-and-thirty years.'

'And when you retired from business you kept all those things?'

'I kept them as some men keep their money, at

compound interest. 'Every year I live increases the value of those things. They belong to manufactures that are extinct. With every year examples perish. Ten years hence the value of my stock will have multiplied by the square of my original capital.'

Mr. Sivewright opened a door on one side of the hall, and, motioning to his guest to follow him, entered a room somewhat brighter of aspect than the hall without. It was a large room, sparsely furnished as to the luxurious appliances of modern homes, but boasting, here and there, in rich relief against the panelled walls, one of those rare and beautiful objects upon which the virtuoso is content to gaze throughout the leisure moments of a lifetime. In the recess on one side of the fireplace stood a noble old buffet, in cherrywood and ebony; in the corresponding recess on the other side a cabinet in Forentine mosaic; from one corner came the solemn tick of an eight-day clock, whose carved and inlaid walnut-wood case was a miracle of art; and upon each central panel of the walls hung a cabinet picture of the Dutch school. So much for the pleasure of the eye. Mere sensual comfort had been less regarded in the arrangement of Mr. Sivewright's sitting-room. A small square of threadbare Persian carpet covered the centre of the oaken floor, serving more for ornament than for luxury.

The rest was bare. A mahogany Pembroke table, value about fifteen shillings, occupied the middle of the room; one shabby-looking arm-chair, horsehair-cushioned, high-backed, and by no means suggestive of repose; two other chairs, of the same family, but without arms; and a business-like deal desk in one of the windows, completed the catalogue of Mr. Sivewright's goods and chattels.

Preparations for dinner, scanty like the furniture, occupied the table; or rather preparations for that joint meal which, in some economic households, combines the feminine refreshment of tea with the more masculine and substantial repast. On one side of the table a small white cloth neatly spread, with a single knife and fork, tumbler, and Venetian flask half-full of claret, indicated that Mr. Sivewright was going to dine: on the other side, a small oval mahogany tray, with a black Wedgewood teapot, suggested that some one else was going to drink tea. A handful of fire burned cheerfully in the wide old-fashioned grate, contracted into the smallest possible compass by checks of firebrick. Throughout the room, scrupulously neat in every detail, Lucius recognised the guiding spirit of parsimony, tempered in all things by some gentler household spirit which contrived to impart some look of comfort even to those meagre surroundings. A pair of candles, not lighted, stood on the table. Mr. Sivewright lighted one of these, and for the first time Lucius was able to see what manner of man his new acquaintance was. All he had been able to discover in the fog was the leonine head and hawk's eye.

The light of the candle showed him a countenance once handsome, but now deeply lined, the complexion dark and sallow, deepening to almost a copper tint in the shadows. The nose aquiline and strongly marked; the upper lip singularly long, the mouth about as indicative of softness or flexibility as if it had been fashioned out of wrought iron; the cheeks worn and hollow; the brow and temples almost hidden by the long loose gray hair, which gave that lion-like aspect to the large head—altogether a face and head to be remembered. The figure tall and spare, but with breadth of shoulder; at times bent, but in some moments of vivacity drawn suddenly erect, as if the man by mere force of will could at pleasure recover the lost energy of his departed youth.

'A curious face,' thought Lucius; 'and there is something in it—something that seems like a memory or an association—which strikes me more forcibly than the face itself. Yet I know not what. I daresay I have dreamed of such a face, or have shaped it in my own fancy to fit some poetic creation—Ugolino, Lear, who knows?'

'Sit down,' said Mr. Sivewright, pointing to a chair opposite his own, into which he had established himself with as comfortable an air as if the chair itself had been the crowning triumph of luxurious upholstery. 'You can drink claret, I suppose?' taking a couple of glasses from the Florentine cabinet, and filling them with the wine on the table. 'I drink no other wine myself. A sound light Medoc, which can hurt nobody.'

'Nobody whose stomach is fortified with a double casing of iron,' thought Lucius, as he sipped the acrid beverage, which he accepted out of courtesy.

'Ten minutes past six,' said Mr. Sivewright, ringing a bell; 'my dinner ought to be on the table.'

An inner door behind Lucius opened as he spoke, and a girl came into the room carrying a little tray, with two small covered dishes. Lucius supposed the new-comer to be a servant, and did not trouble himself to look up till she had placed her dishes on the table, and lingered to give the finishing touches to the arrangement of the board. He did look up then, and saw that this ministering spirit was no common hireling, but one of the most interesting women he had ever seen.

She was hardly to be called a woman; she was but in the opening blossom of girlhood; a fragile-looking flower, pale as some waxen-petalled exotic reared under glass, with the thermometer at seventy-six. She had something foreign, or even tropical, in her appearance; eyes dark as night, hair of the same sombre hue. Her figure was of middle height, slim, but with no sharpness of outline; every curve perfection, every line grace. Her features were delicately pencilled, but not strikingly beautiful. Indeed, the chief and all-pervading charm of her appearance was that exquisite delicacy, that flower-like fragility which moved one to exclaim, 'How lovely, but how short-lived!'

Yet it is not always these delicate blossoms which fade the first; the tough-stemmed poppy will sometimes be mown down by Death's inexorable sickle, while the opal-hued petals of the dog-rose still breast the storm. There was a strength of endurance beneath this fragile exterior which Lucius would have been slow to believe in.

The girl glanced at the stranger with much surprise, but without the slightest embarrassment. Rarely did a stranger sit beside that hearth. But there had been such intruders from time to time, traders or clients of the old man's. She had no curiosity upon the subject.

'Your dinner is quite ready, grandfather,' she said; 'you had better eat it before it grows cold.'

She lifted the covers from the two dainty little dishes—a morsel of steak cooked in some foreign fashion—a handful of sliced potato fried in oil.

Lucius rose to depart.

'I won't intrude upon you any longer, Mr. Sivewright,' he said; 'but if you will allow me to call upon you some day and look at your wonderful collection, I shall be very glad.'

'Stay where you are,' answered the other in his authoritative way; 'you've dined, I've no doubt.' A convenient way of settling *that* question. 'Lucille, my granddaughter, can give you a cup of tea.'

Lucille smiled, with a little gesture of assent strikingly foreign, Lucius thought. An English girl would hardly have been so gracious to a nameless stranger.

'I told you, when we first met in that abominable fog, that I liked your voice,' said Mr. Sivewright. 'I'll go farther now, and say I like your face. I forgive you your profession, as I said before. Stay, and see my collection to-night.'

'That is as much as to say, "See all you want

to see to-night, and don't plague me with **any future visits,"**' thought Lucius, who found **that meagrely-**furnished room, that scanty fire, more attractive since the appearance of Lucille.

He accepted the invitation, however; drew his chair to the tea-table, and drank two cups of tea and ate two or three small slices of bread-and-butter with **a** sublime disregard **of the fact** that he **had** not broken his fast since eight o'clock in the morning. He had acquired a passion for mild decoctions of congou **in those** days of privation far away beyond the Saskat-**chewan;** and this particular tea seemed **to have a** subtle aroma which made it better than any **he had** ever brewed **for** himself beside his solitary hearth.

'I became a tea-drinker four years ago, in the Far West,' he said, as an excuse for his second cup.

' Do you mean in America?' the girl asked eagerly.

'Yes. Have you **ever been over yonder ?**'

'Never; **only** I am always interested **in** hearing of America.'

' You had much better be interested in hearing of the **moon,'** said Mr. Sivewright, **with an angry look**; ' **you are** just as likely to discover anything there that **concerns you.'**

' **You have relations or friends** in America, perhaps, Miss Sivewright?' inquired **Lucius; but a little** warning look and gesture from Lucille prevented his repeating the question.

He began to tell her some of his adventures beyond the Red River—not his hours of dire strait and calamity, not the horror of his forest experiences. Those were things he never spoke of, scenes he dared not think of, days which it was misery to him to remember.

'You must have gone through great hardship,' she said, after listening to him with keen interest. 'Were you never in actual peril?'

'Once. We were lost in a forest westward of the Rocky Mountains. But that is a period I do not care to speak of. My dearest friend was ill—at the point of death. Happily for us a company of Canadian emigrants, bound for the gold-fields, came across our track just in time to save us. But for that providential circumstance I shouldn't be here to tell you the story. Wolves or wolverines would have picked my bones.'

'Horrible!' exclaimed Lucille, with a shudder.

'Yes. Wolves are not agreeable society. But human nature is still more horrible when it casts off the mask of civilisation.'

Mr. Sivewright had finished his dinner by this time, and had absorbed two glasses of the sound

Medoc without a single contortion of his visage; a striking instance of the force of habit.

'Come,' said he. 'I'll show you some of my collection. You're no judge of art, I suppose. I never knew a young man who was; though they're always ready enough with their opinions.'

He took up one of the candles, and led the way to the hall, thence to a room on the other side of the house, larger than the family sitting-room, and used as a storehouse for his treasures. Here Lucius beheld the same confusion of bric-à-brac which had bewildered him on his first entrance into that singular mansion, only on a larger scale. Pictures again, statues again, cabinets, tables, fragmentary pieces of mediæval oak carving, stray panels that had once lined old Flemish churches, choir-stalls with sacred story carved upon their arms and backs; armour again, grim and ghastly as the collection of the Hôtel Cluny, demonstrating how man's invention, before it entered the vast field of gunnery, had lavished its wanton cruelty on forms that hack and hew, and jag and tear and saw; spiky swords, pole-axes with serrated edges, pikes from which dangled iron balls studded with sharp points; and so on. Ceramic ware, again, of every age, from a drinking-vessel dug from beneath one of the earth-mounds on the shores of the

Euphrates to the chocolatière out of which Marie Jeanne Vaubernier, otherwise Du Barri, took her last breakfast. And, rising grim above the frivolities of art, loomed the gaunt outline of a Scottish Maiden, the rough germ of the Gallic guillotine.

The old man looked round his storehouse with a smile of triumph, holding aloft his single candle, every object showing strangely, and casting uncanny shadows in that feeble light, he himself not the least curious figure in the Rembrandtesque picture. He looked like some enchanter, who, at a breath, had called these things into being.

'You astound me!' exclaimed Lucius, looking about him with unaffected wonder. 'You spoke some time ago of having saved the remnant of your stock; but you have here a collection larger than I should have supposed any dealer in curiosities would care to amass, even in the full swing of his business.'

'Perhaps,' answered Mr. Sivewright with a dreamy air. 'For the mere purposes of trade—for trade upon the nimble-ninepence system—there is no doubt too much. But these things have accumulated since I left off business. The passion for collecting them was not to be put away as easily as I put up my shutters with the expiry of a long lease. My harpy of a landlord asked a rent so exorbitant, that I preferred cutting short a successful trade to pandering to his greed. True that the situation **had** increased in value during the last twenty-one years of my residence; but I declined to toil for another **man's profit. I turned my back** upon Bond-street, determined to take life quietly in future. I found this old house—to be let cheap, and roomy enough to hold my treasures. Since that time I have amused myself by attending all the great sales, and a good many of the little ones. I have been to Paris, Brussels, Antwerp—and farther afield—on **special occasions.** My collection has grown upon me—it **represents** all I possess in the world, all that I can **ever** leave to my descendants. As I told you, I anticipate that as the value of money decreases, and the **age** grows more artistic, the value of these specimens, all relics of departed arts, will be multiplied fourfold.'

'A wise investment, in that case,' replied Lucius; 'but if the age should have touched its highest point of luxurious living, if the passion for splendid **surroundings,** once the attribute only of a Buckingham or a Hertford, now the vice **of the** million, should work its **own** cure, and give place to a Spartan **simplicity, how then?'**

'My collection would most likely be purchased **by the State,' said the old man** coolly; 'a destiny which I should infinitely prefer to its disintegration, however profitable. *Then*, Mr. Davoren, the name of Homer Sivewright would go down to posterity linked with one of the noblest Museums ever created by a single individual.'

'Pardon me,' said Lucius; 'but your name Homer—is that a family or merely a Christian name?'

'The name given me by my foolish old father—whose father was a contemporary of Bentley—who gave his life to the study of Homer, and tried to establish the thesis that early Greece had but one poet; that the cyclic poets were the merest phantasma; and that Stasinus, Arctinus, Lesches, and the rest, were but the mouthpieces of that one mighty bard. Every man is said to be mad upon one point, or mad once in twenty-four hours. My father was very mad about Greek. He gave me my ridiculous name —which made me the laughing-stock of my schoolfellows—a university education and his blessing. He had no more to give. My college career cost him the only fortune he could have left me; and I found myself, at one-and-twenty, fatherless, motherless, homeless, and penniless, and—what to my poor father would have seemed worst of all—plucked for my incapacity to appreciate the niceties of Homeric Greek.'

'How did you weather the storm?'

'I might not have weathered it at all, but for a self-delusion which sustained me in the very face of starvation. But for that I could hardly have crossed Waterloo-bridge without being sorely tempted to take the shortest cut out of my perplexities. I fancied myself a painter. That dream kept me alive. I got bread somehow; sold my daubs to a dealer; made some progress even in the art of daubing; and only after five years of hard work and harder living awoke one day to the bitter truth that I was no more a painter than I was a Grecian, no nearer Reynolds than Porson.'

'You bore your disappointment bravely, I imagine.'

'Why imagine that?'

'Because your physiognomy teaches me your ability to come safely through such an ordeal—a will strong enough to stand against even a worse shock.'

'You are right. I parted with my delusion quietly enough, though it had brightened my boyhood, and kept me alive during five weary years. As I could not be a painter of pictures, I determined to be a dealer in them, and began life once more in a little den of a shop, in a court near Leicester-square—began with ten pounds for my capital; bought a bit of old china for three-and-sixpence, and sold it for ten shillings; had an occasional stroke of luck as time went by; once picked up a smoke-darkened picture of a piggery, which turned out an indisputable Morland; went everywhere and saw everything that was to be seen in the shape of pictures and ceramic ware; lived in an atmosphere of art, and brought to bear upon my petty trade a genuine passion for art, which stood me in good stead against bigwigs whose knowledge was only technical. In four years I had a stock worth three thousand pounds, and was able to open a shop in Bond-street. A man with a window in Bond-street must be an arrant ass if he can't make money. The dilettanti found me out, and discovered that I had received the education of a gentleman. Young men about town made my shop a lounge. I sold them the choicest brands of cigars, under the rose, and occasionally lent them money; for which I charged them about half the interest they would have paid a professed usurer. My profits were reinvested in fresh stock as fast as they accumulated. I acquired a reputation for judgment and taste; and, in a word, I succeeded; which I should never have done had I insisted upon thinking myself a neglected Raphael.'

'I thank you for your history, more interesting

to my mind than any object in your collection. I do not wonder that you were loth to part with the gems of art you had slowly gathered. But had none of your children the inclination to continue so fascinating a trade?'

'My children!' repeated Homer Sivewright, with a gloomy look; 'I have no children. When you talk to a stranger, Mr. Davoren, beware of commonplace questions. They sometimes gall a raw spot.'

'Pardon me; only seeing that interesting young lady—your granddaughter—'

'That granddaughter represents all my kindred upon earth. I *had* a son—that girl's father. But there is not a figure carved on yonder oaken choir-stalls of less account to me than that son is now.'

Lucius was silent. He had been unlucky enough to stumble upon the threshold of a family mystery. Yes, he had fancied some touch of sadness, some vague shadow of a quiet grief, in that sweet young face. The child of a disgraced father; her gentle spirit even yet weighed down by the memory of some ancient shame. He thought of the sorrow that had darkened his own youth—the bitter memory which haunted him even yet — the memory of his lost sister.

He went through the collection, seeing things as

well as he could by the light of a solitary candle. Mr. Sivewright displayed his various treasures with infinite enthusiasm; dilating upon the modelling here, the colouring there; through all the technicalities of art. He kept his guest absorbed in this investigation for nearly two hours, although there were moments when the younger man's thoughts wandered back to the parlour where they had left Lucille.

He was thinking of her even while he appeared to listen with intense interest to Mr. Sivewright's explanation of the difference between *pâte tendre* and *pâte dure;* wondering if she lived alone in that huge rambling house with her grandfather, like little Nell in the *Old Curiosity Shop;* only it was to be hoped with no such diabolical familiar as Quilp privileged to intrude upon her solitude. So anxious was he to be satisfied on this point, that he ventured to ask the question, despite his previous ill-fortune.

'Yes,' answered Mr. Sivewright coolly, 'we live quite alone. Dull, you'll say, perhaps, for my granddaughter. If it is, she must resign herself to circumstances. There are worse things to bear than want of company. If she hadn't this home, she'd have none. Well, I suppose you've seen as many of these things as you care about. I can see your mind's wandering. So we may as well bid each other good-night. I'm obliged to you for your civility this afternoon. This way.'

He opened the door into the hall. A somewhat abrupt dismissal, and one Lucius had not expected. He had reckoned upon finishing his evening far more pleasantly in the society of Lucille.

'I should like to bid Miss Sivewright good-evening,' he said.

'There's no occasion. I can do it for you. There's your hat, on the black-marble slab yonder,' said the old man, seeing his visitor looking round in search of that article, with a faint hope that he might have left it in the parlour.

'Thanks. But I hope you don't forbid my coming to see you again sometimes?' Lucius asked bluntly.

'Humph!' muttered the old man, 'it would sound ungracious to talk of forbidding any future visit. But I have lived in this house five years, and have not made an acquaintance. One of the chief attractions of this place, to my mind, was the fact that it was cut off by a ten-foot wall from the world outside. With every wish to be civil, I can't see why I should make an exception in your favour. Besides, you've seen all there is worth seeing within these walls; you could have no possible pleasure in coming to us. We are poor, and we live poorly.'

'I am not a seeker of wealthy acquaintance. A quiet fireside—an atmosphere of home—brightened by the refinements of art; that is what I should value above all things in a house where I was free to visit; and that your house could give me. But if you say No, I submit. I cannot force myself upon you.'

'I have a granddaughter who will be penniless if she offends me,' said the old man, with the same gloomy look which had darkened his face when he spoke of his son. 'I do not care for any strange influence to come between us. As it is, we are happy —not loving each other in any silly romantic fashion, but living together in mutual endurance. No; I should be a fool to admit any disturbing element.'

'Be it so,' said Lucius. 'I am a struggling man, and have hardly trodden the first stage of an uphill journey. The friendship I offer is not worth much.'

'I should refuse it in exactly the same manner if you were a millionnaire,' answered the other, opening the heavy old door, and admitting the fog. He led the way across the forecourt, unlocked the tall iron gate, and his visitor passed out into the sordid realities of the Shadrack-road.

'Once more, good-night,' said Mr. Sivewright.

'Good-night,' answered Lucius, as the gate closed

upon him, with a creak like the caw of an **evil-minded raven.** He **turned** his face homeward, intensely mortified. He **was a** proud man, and **had** offered **his** friendship **to a** retired bric-à-brac dealer, **only** to have it flatly rejected. But it was not **wounded** pride which vexed him as he **walked home** through the fog.

'There's no **such** thing as **love at first sight,**' he said to himself; 'yet when a man has lived for half-a-dozen years without seeing a pretty face in his own rank of life, his heart is apt to be rather inflam**mable.**'

CHAPTER III.

HARD HIT.

Lucius Davoren found himself curiously disturbed by the memory of that pretty face in his own rank of life—that glimpse of a fireside different from the common firesides of the Shadrack-Basin district—the fat and prosperous hearths, where the atmosphere was odorous with tea, shrimps, muffins, and gin-and-water; the barren hearth-stoves by which destitution hugged itself in its rags. He went about his daily work with his accustomed earnestness, was no whit the less tender to the little children, watched with the same anxious care by pauper sick beds, handled shattered limbs or loathsome sores with the same gentle touch; in a word, did his duty thoroughly, in this dismal, initiative stage of his career.

But he never passed Cedar House without a regretful sigh and a lingering gaze at its blank upper windows; which, showing no trace of the life within, had a wall-eyed look that was worse than the utter blindness of closed shutters. He sometimes went out of his way even, for the sake of passing those inexorable walls. He wasted a few minutes of his busy day loitering by the iron gate, hoping that by some kindly caprice of Fortune the pale sweet face of Lucille Sivewright would appear behind the rusty bars, the ponderous hinge would creak, and the girl who haunted his thoughts would emerge from her gloomy prison.

'Does she never come out?' he asked himself one fine winter day, when there was sunshine even in the realms of Shadrack. It was a month after his adventure with Homer Sivewright, and he had lingered by the gate a good many times. 'Does she never breathe the free air of heaven, never see the faces of mankind? Is she a cloistered nun in all but the robe, and without the companionship which may make a convent tolerable?—without even the affection of that grim old grandfather? for how coldly he spoke of her! What a life!'

Lucius was full of pity for this girl, whom he had only known one brief hour. If any one had suggested that he was in love with her, he would have scorned the notion. Yet there are passions which endure for a lifetime; which defy death and blossom above a grave; though their history may be reckoned by rare hours of brightness, too easily reckoned in the dull sum of life.

'Love at sight is but the fancy of poets and fools,' thought Lucius; 'but it would be strange if I were not sorry for a fair young life thus blighted.'

His violin had a new pathos for him now, in those occasional hours of leisure when he laid aside his books and opened the case which held that magician. His favourite sonatas breathed a languid melancholy, which sounded to him like the complaint of an imprisoned soul—that princess of fairy tale—the bric-à-brac dealer's granddaughter. But to think of her thus, as he played dreamily by his lonely fireside, was only to feel a natural compassion for an oppressed fellow-creature.

This tendency to dwell upon one subject, and that a foolish one, since his pity could not be of the smallest service to its object, finally worried him not a little. Thus it was that, finding himself his own master an hour or so earlier than usual one January afternoon, he told himself that the wisest thing he could do would be to get away from the Shadrack-road atmosphere altogether.

'The life I lead is too narrow, too completely monotonous,' he thought. 'No wonder I have taken to exaggerate the importance of trifles. Yes, I will refresh myself by a few hours' liberty in a brighter world. I will go and hunt up Geoffrey Hossack.'

They were firm friends still, though their lives lay as wide apart as two rivers which have their source from the same watershed, and wander off by opposite ways to the sea, never to touch again. They had lost sight of each other for some time of late. Geoffrey, ever a peripatetic spirit, had been doing Norway, with an excursus into Lapland during the last two years; but a letter received just before Christmas had announced his return, and his sojourn at a manor-house in Yorkshire.

'I shall begin the new year in the City of cities,' he wrote; 'and one of my first occupations will be to beat up your quarters in that queer world of yours beyond the Tower. But if you are kind enough to forestall me, you will find me in my old rooms at Philpott's.—Yours, as per usual, **G. H.**'

The new year had begun, and had brought no sign from Geoffrey; so Lucius took advantage of his leisure to go westward in quest of his friend. He detested the slow tortures of an omnibus, and was too poor to afford himself a hansom; so he gave himself the luxury of a walk.

That journey took him almost from one end of London to the other. The forest of spars, the ropewalk, the open gates of the docks, the perpetual procession of hogsheads, cotton bales, iron bars, packing-cases, and petroleum barrels, gave place to the crowded streets of the City, where all the operations of commerce seemed to be carried on quietly, by men who walked to and fro, carrying no merchandise, but buying and selling as it were by sign and countersign. Then came that borderland on the westward side of Temple Bar—that somewhat shabby and doubtful region where loom the churches of St. Clement and St. Mary, which seem to have been especially designed as perpetual standing impediments to the march of architectural progress in this quarter; then the brighter shop-windows and more holiday air of the western Strand; and then Charing-cross; and a little way farther on, hanging-on to the skirts of Pall Mall and the Clubs, behold Philpott's or the Cosmopolitan Hotel, an old-fashioned house with a narrow façade in red-brick, pinched-in between its portlier neighbours—a house which looked small, but boasted of making up forty beds, and retaining all the year round a staff of thirty servants.

Mr. Hossack was at home. The waiter of whom Lucius asked the question brightened at the sound of his name, as if he had been a personal friend, and took Lucius under his protection on the instant.

'This way, sir; the first-floor. Mr. Hossack has his own particular rooms here. We once refused them to a Cabinet Minister, because Mr. Hossack wanted them.'

'A general favourite, I suppose.'

'Lord bless you, sir, down to the vegetable maid, we worship him.'

The enthusiastic waiter opened a door, and ushered in the guest. There had been no question as to card or name. Geoffrey Hossack was accessible as the sunshine.

He was half buried in a low capacious chair, his head flung back on the cushions, a cigar between his lips, an open French novel flung face downwards on the carpet beside him, amongst a litter of newspapers. The winter dusk had almost deepened into night, and the room was unlighted save by the fire. Yet even in that fitful light Lucius saw that his friend's countenance was moody; a fact so rare as to awaken curiosity, or even concern.

'Geoff, old fellow!'

'Why, Davoren!' cried Geoffrey, starting up from his luxurious repose, and flinging the unfinished cigar into the fire. 'How good of you! And I ought to have come to your place. I've been in London a fortnight.'

'My dear old boy, one hardly expects Alcibiades beyond the Minories. I have been living at that dingy end of town until to come westward is a new sensation. When I saw Trafalgar-square and the lighted windows of yonder Club to-night, I felt like Columbus when he sighted the coast of San Salvador. I had a leisure afternoon, and thought I couldn't spend it better than in looking you up. And now, Geoff, for your Norwegian and Laplandian experiences. You were looking uncommonly gloomy when I came in; as if your memories of the north were not of the brightest.'

'My northern memories are pleasant enough,' said the other, putting aside the question lightly, just in that old familiar way Lucius knew so well. 'Come, Lucius, plant yourself there,' rolling over another capacious chair, the last device of some satanic upholsterer for the propagation of slothful habits; 'take one of those Havanas, and light up. I can never talk freely to a man till I can hardly see his face across the clouds of his tobacco—a native modesty of disposition, I suppose; or perhaps that disinclination to look my fellow-man straight in the face which is accounted one of the marks of a villanous character. Goodish weed, isn't it? Do you remember British Columbia, Davoren, and the long days and nights when there **was no tobacco?**'

'Do I remember?' echoed the surgeon, **looking at the** fire. 'Am I ever likely to forget?'

'Of course not. **The** question was a mere *façon de parler*. There are things that no man can forget. Can I forget, for instance, how you saved my life? how through **all** those wearisome nights and days when I was lying rolled up in **my** buffalo skins raving like a lunatic, fancying myself in all sorts of places and among all sorts of people, you were **at** once doctor and sick-nurse, guardian and provider?'

'**Please don't talk** of that time, Geoff. There are some things better forgotten. I did no more for **you** than I'd have done for a stranger; except that my heart went with my service, and would have almost broken if you had **died.** Our sufferings and our peril at that time seem to me too bitter even **for** remembrance. I can't endure to look back at them.'

'Strange!' exclaimed Geoffrey lightly. 'To **me they** afford an unfailing source of satisfaction. I rarely order a dinner without thinking of the days when my vital powers were sustained—"sustained" is hardly the word, say rather "suspended"—by mouldy pemmican. I seldom open a new **box of** cigars without remembering those doleful hours in which I smoked dried grass, flavoured with the last scrapings of nicotine from my meerschaum. It is the converse of what somebody says about a sorrow's crown of sorrow. The memory of past hardship sweetens the comfort of the present. But I do shudder sometimes when I remember awakening from *my* delirium to find *you* down with brain-fever, and poor little Schanck sitting awe-stricken by your side, like a man who had been holding converse with spirits. I don't mean schnapps, but something uncanny. Thank God, those Canadian emigrants found us out soon afterwards, or He only knows how our story would have ended.'

'Thank God!' echoed Lucius solemnly. 'I know nothing of my illness, can remember nothing till I found myself strapped like a bundle upon a horse's back, riding through the snow.'

'We moved you before you were quite right in your head,' answered Geoffrey apologetically. 'The Canadians wouldn't wait any longer. It was our only chance of being put into the right track.'

'You did a wise thing, Geoff. It was good for me to wake up far from that wretched log-hut.'

'Come now, after all, we had some very jolly times there,' said Geoffrey, with his habit of making the best of life; 'sitting by the blazing pine-logs jawing away like old boots. It was only when our 'baccy ran out that existence became a burden. I give you my honour that sometimes when civilised life begins to hang heavy, I look back to the days when we crossed the Rocky Mountains with a regretful sigh. I almost envy that plucky little German sea-captain who left us at Victoria, and went on to San Francisco to dig for gold.'

'I verily believe, Geoff, you would have contrived to be cheerful in the Black Hole at Calcutta, or on the middle passage. You have a limitless reserve fund of animal spirits.'

'There you're wrong. I believed as much myself till the other day. But I have lately discovered a latent faculty hitherto unsuspected even by myself; the capacity for being miserable.'

'You have sustained some family affliction,—or you have taken to wearing tight boots?'

'Neither. I wish you'd help yourself to some brandy-and-soda yonder,' interjected Mr. Hossack, pointing to a side-table on which those refreshments were provided, and ringing the bell clamorously; 'I'll order dinner before I unbosom myself. George,' to the enthusiastic waiter, who appeared in prompt answer to the noisy summons, 'the best you can do for this gentleman and me, at seven sharp; and don't come fidgeting in and out to lay the cloth until five minutes before you bring the soup tureen. By the way, we'll begin with oysters and Montrachet, and you can give us a bottle of Yquem afterwards. No sparkling wine. We'll wind up with Chambertin, if you've a bottle in good condition. But don't bring it half-frozen out of the cellar, or muddled by hasty thawing. Exercise judgment, George; you have to deal with connoisseurs. Now,' continued this epicurean youth, flinging himself back into the depths of his chair, 'before I begin my egotistical prosing, let me hear what you've been doing all this time, my Lucius.'

'That may be told in two words. Hard work.'

'Poor old Davoren!'

'Don't take that simple statement as a complaint. It is work I like. I might have set up my Penates in what is called a genteel neighbourhood, and earned my crust a good deal more easily than I can earn it yonder. But I wanted wide experience—a complete initiation—and I went where humanity is thickest. The result has more than satisfied me. If ever I move westward it will be to Savile-row.'

The sybarite contemplated his friend admiringly, yet with a stifled yawn, as if the very contemplation of so much vital force were fatiguing.

'Upon my word, I don't know that I wouldn't exchange my three-per-cents for your ambition, Lucius,' he said. 'To have something to achieve, something to win—that is the keenest rapture of the human mind, that makes the chief delight of the chase. Upon my honour, I envy you. I seem to awake to the conviction that it is a misfortune to be born with the proverbial silver spoon in one's mouth.'

'The man who begins life with a fortune starts ahead of the penniless struggler in the race for fame,' answered the surgeon. 'There is plenty of scope for your ambition, Geoff, in spite of the three-per-cents.'

'What could I do?'

'Try to make yourself famous.'

'Not possible! Unless I took to a pea-green coat, like that rich young West Indian swell in the last generation. Fame! bah! for Brown, Jones, or Robinson to talk of making themselves famous is about as preposterous as it would be for Hampstead-hill to try and develop a volcano. Men born to fame have a special brand upon their foreheads, like the stamp on Veuve Clicquot's champagne corks. I think I see it in the anxious lines that mark yours, Lucius.'

'There is the senate,' said Davoren; 'the natural aim of an Englishman's ambition.'

'What! truckle to rural shopkeepers for the privilege of wasting the summer evenings and the spring tides in a stuffy manufactory of twaddle. *Pas si bête!*'

'After all,' returned Lucius, with a faint sigh, 'you have something better than ambition, which is only life in the future—mere fetish worship, perhaps—or the adoration of a shadow which may never become a substance. You have youth, and the power to enjoy all youth's pleasures; that is to say, life in the present.'

'So I thought till very lately,' answered Geoffrey, with another sigh; 'but there is a new flavour of bitterness in the wine of life. Lucius, I'm going to ask you a serious question. Do you believe in love at first sight?'

A startling question at any rate, for it brought the blood into the surgeon's toil-worn face. Happily they were still sitting in the firelight, which just now waxed dim.

'About as much as I believe in ghosts or spirit-rapping,' he answered coldly.

'Which means that you've never seen a ghost or had a message from spirit-land,' answered Geoffrey. 'Six months ago I should have called any one an ass who could love a woman of whom he knew no more than that her face was lovely and her voice divine. But as somebody—a baker's daughter, wasn't she?—

observed, "We know what we are, but we know not what we may be."'

'You have fallen in love, Geoff?'

'Descended into abysmal depths of folly, a million fathoms below the soundings of common sense. There's nothing romantic in the business either, which of course makes it worse. It's only foolish. I didn't save the lady's life; by stopping a pair of horses that were galloping to perdition with her; or by swimming out a mile or so to snatch her from the devouring jaws of an ebb tide. I have no excuse for my madness. The lady is a concert-singer, and I first saw her while dancing attendance upon some country cousins who were staying in town the other day, and led me like a victim to musical mornings and evening recitals, and so on. You know that I have not a passionate love of music.'

'I know that you had a very moderate appreciation of my violin.'

'All the tunes sounded so much alike. Want of taste on my part, of course. However, my cousins —Arabella and Jessie, nice girls, but domineering—insisted that I should go to concerts, so I went. They both sing and play, and wanted to improve their style, they said; selfishly ignoring the fact that I had no style to improve; and allowing me to pay for all the tickets. One morning—splendid weather for snowballing; I wished myself young again and at Winchester, as I looked at the streets—we went to a Recital, which took place in a dreary-looking house near Manchester-square, by the kind permission of the tenant. The concert people might as well have borrowed a roomy family vault. It would have been quite as cheerful. Well, we surrendered our tickets—parallelograms of sky-blue pasteboard, and uncommonly dear at half a guinea—to a shabby footman, who ushered us up-stairs over a threadbare stair carpet to a faded drawing-room, where we found some elderly ladies of the dowdy order, and a miscellaneous collection of antique gentlemen in well-worn coats of exploded cut. These I took to represent the musical nobility. It was not a cheerful concert. First came a quartette, in ever so many parts, like a dull sermon; a quartette for a piano, violoncello, and two fiddles, with firstly, and secondly, and thirdly. Every now and then, when the violoncello gave forth rather deeper groans than usual, or one of the fiddles prolonged a wire-drawn note, the musical nobility gave a little gasp, and looked at one another, and one of the old gentlemen tapped the lid of his snuffbox. After the quartette we had a pianoforte solo, to my unenlightened mind an arid waste of tuneless chords, and little meandering runs to nowhere in particular, a little less interesting than a problem in Euclid. I prefer my cousin Arabella's hearty thumping, and frantic rushes up and down the keyboard, to this milk-and-water style, which is, I understand, classical. Number three was a vocal duet by Handel, which I won't describe, as it lulled me into a placid slumber. When I reopened my eyes there was a gentle murmur of admiration floating in the atmosphere; and I beheld a lady dressed in black, with a sheet of music in her hand, waiting for the end of the symphony.'

'*The* lady, I suppose,' said Lucius, duly interested.

'The lady. I won't attempt to describe her; for after all what can one say of the loveliest woman except that she has a straight nose, fine eyes, a good complexion? And yet these constitute so small a part of Beauty. One may see them in the street every day. This one stood there like a statue in the cold wintry light, and seemed to me the most perfect being I had ever beheld. She appeared divinely unconscious of her beauty, as unconscious as Aphrodite must have been in that wild free world of newborn Greece, though all creation worshipped her. She didn't look about her with a complacent smile, challenging admiration. Her dark-fringed eyelids drooped over the violet-gray eyes, as she looked downward at the music. Her dress was Quaker-like, a linen collar round the full firm throat, the perfect arm defined by the plain black sleeve. Art had done nothing to enhance or to detract from her beauty. She sang "Auld Robin Gray" in a voice that went to my inmost heart. The musical nobility sniffed and murmured rapturously. The old gentleman rapped his snuffbox, and said Bwava! and the song was re-demanded. She curtsied and began something about a blue bodice and Lubin, and in this there were bird-like trills, and a prolonged shake, clear and strong as the carol of a sky-lark. Lucius, I was such a demented ass at that moment, that if the restraints of civilisation hadn't been uncommonly strong upon me, I should have wept like a schoolboy before a caning.'

'Something in the *timbre* of the voice,' said Lucius, ' simpatica.'

'Sim-anybody you like; it knocked me over as if I'd been a skittle.'

'Have you seen her since?'

'Have I seen her! I have followed her from concert-room to concert-room, until my *sensorium*—that's the word, isn't it?—aches from the amount of classical music that has been inflicted upon it—the x minors and z majors, and so forth. Sometimes I hunted her down in some other aristocratic drawing-room, by the kind permission, &c.; sometimes I found her at the Hanover-square Rooms. Mitchell has a standing order to send me a ticket for every concert at which she sings. It's deuced hard work. I'm due this time to-morrow at St. George's Hall, Liverpool.'

'But, my dear old Geoff, can anything be more foolish?' expostulated Lucius, forgetful of that rusty old gate in the Shadrack-road, to which purest pity had so often led him.

'I daresay not. But I can't help myself.'

'Do you know anything about the lady?'

'All that a diligent process of private inquiry could discover; and yet very little. The lady is a widow—'

'Disenchanting fact.'

'Her name, Bertram.'

'Assumed, no doubt.'

'Very possibly. She has lodgings in Keppel-street, Russell-square, and lives a life of extreme seclusion with one little girl. I saw the child one morning, a seraph of seven or eight, with flowing flaxen hair, blue frock, and scarlet legs, like a tropical bird, or a picture by Millais.'

'That sounds like respectability.'

'Respectability!' cried Geoffrey, flaming with indignation. 'I would no more doubt her honour than I would question that of my dead mother. If you had heard her sing "Voi che sapéte," the clear thrilling tones, now swelling into a flood of melody, now sinking to the tenderest whisper! Could such tones as those come from an impure heart? No, Lucius. I need no certificate of character to tell me that Jane Bertram is true.'

Lucius smiled—the slow smile of worldly wisdom—and then breathed a faint regretful sigh for his friend's delusion.

'My dear Geoff,' he said,' 'I daresay the conclusion you arrive at is natural to the unsophisticated mind. A great orator addresses us like a demigod; ergo, he must be by nature godlike. Yet his life may be no better than Thurlow's or Wilkes's. A woman is divinely beautiful; and we argue that her soul, too, must be divine. The history of the musical stage tells us that in days gone by there were women who sang like angels, yet were by no means perfect as women. For God's sake, dear old friend, beware of music. Of all man's ensnarers the siren with lyre and voice is the most dangerous. Of all woman's tempters he who breathes his earthly desires in heavenly-sounding melody is the most fatal. In my own family there has been a wretched **example of this** nature. I speak with all the bitterness that comes from bitter experience.'

'That may **be so**,' returned the other, unconvinced; 'but there are instincts which cannot lie. **My** belief **in Jane Bertram is** fixed as the sun in heaven.'

'Did you contrive to obtain an introduction?'

'**No.** I found that impossible. She knows no **one,** goes nowhere, except for her professional engagements. Even the people **who** engage her — music publishers, and what not — know nothing about her; except that she sings better than five out of six sopranos of established reputation, and that she has struggled into her present modest position out of obscurity and hard work. She was only a teacher of music until very lately. She would do wonders if she went on the stage, my informant told me; and such a course was suggested to her; but **she** peremptorily declined to entertain the idea. **She** earns, in the season, about five pounds a-week. What a pittance for a goddess!'

'And who was Mr. Bertram?'

'I was not curious upon that subject; enough for me to know that he is in his **grave. But had**

I been ever so inquisitive my curiosity must have gone unsatisfied. The people who know so little about her know still less about her late husband. He has been dead some years. That is all they could tell me.'

'And you positively go down to Liverpool to hear her sing!'

'As I would go back to the shores of the Red River for the same purpose. Ay, live again on mouldy pemmican, and hear again the howling of the wolves at sunset.'

'And is this kind of thing to go on indefinitely?'

'It will go on until circumstances favour my passion, until I can win my way to her friendship, to her confidence; until I can say to her, without fear of repulse or discouragement, "Jane, I love you." I am quite content to serve a longish apprenticeship, even to classical music, for the sake of that reward.'

Lucius stretched out his hand, and the two men's broad palms met in the grasp of friendship.

'Upon my honour, Geoffrey, I admire you,' said the surgeon. 'I won't preach any more. Granted that your passion is foolish, at least it's thorough. I honour a man who can say to himself, "That woman I will marry, and no other; that woman I will follow, through honour and dishonour, evil report and good report—"'

'Stop,' cried Geoffrey; 'let there be no mention of dishonour in the same breath with her name. If I did not believe in her truth and purity, I would pluck this passion out of my breast—as the Carthusian prior in the mediæval legend plucked deadly sin out of the entrails of St. Hugo of Lincoln—though I cut my heart open to do it. I love her, and I believe in her.'

'And if you ceased to believe in her, you would cease to love her?'

'Yes,' answered Geoffrey Hossack firmly.

He had risen from his seat by the hearth, and was pacing the dusky chamber, where the street lamps without and the red fire within made a curious half-light. Truly had his friend called him thorough. Intense, passionate, and impulsive was this generous nature—a nature which had never been spoiled by that hard school in which all men must learn whose first necessity is to get their living, that dreary breadwinner's academical career to which God condemned Adam as the direst punishment of his disobedience and deceit. 'No longer shalt thou wander careless in these flowery vales and groves, where generous emotions and affectionate impulses and noble thoughts might bud and blossom in the happy idlesse. For thee, sinner, the daily round of toil, the constant hurry, the ever-goading pressure of sordid necessities, which shall make thee selfish and hard and remorseless, with no leisure in which to be kind to thy brother strugglers, with hardly a pause in which to remember thy God!'

CHAPTER IV.

'O WORLD, HOW APT THE POOR ARE TO BE PROUD!'

Lucius thought much of his friend after that frank confession at the Cosmopolitan. Geoffrey had dined none the less well because of his passion. He had eaten oysters, and bisque soup, and stewed calves' head with truffles, and mutton, and wild duck, with the appetite that had been educated in an American pine-forest; had drunk Château d'Yquem, and Chambertin, and wound up with curaçoa, and had waxed merry to riotousness as the evening grew late,—Lucius taking but a moderate share in the revel, yet enjoying it. Was it not a glimpse of a new life, after the Shadrack-road, where pleasure had a universal flavour of gin-and-water?

They parted after midnight with warm protestations of friendship. They were to see each other again. Geoffrey was to look his friend up in the Shadrack district as soon as his engagements permitted. But wherever *she* went, he would follow her, were it to that possible continent or archipelago at the southern pole.

So Lucius went back to the region of many spars and much rigging, and solaced his lonely evenings with the pensive strains of his violin, and pondered long and gravely upon that wondrous mystery of love which could befool even so healthy a nature as that of honest, open-hearted, plain-spoken Geoffrey Hossack. Love allied with music! 'Yes,' he thought, as he sighed over the long-drawn chords of an adagio, '*that* is the fatal witchcraft.'

Anon came February, season of sleet and east winds, the month in which winter—after seeming, towards the end of January, to have grown genial and temperate, with even faint whispers of coming spring—generally undergoes a serious relapse, and plunges anew into hyperborean darkness, fog, tempest, snow. Lucius had passed the old house in the Shadrack-road almost every day since November (even when it lay out of his beat he contrived to walk that way), but had seen no more sign of human life about that dismal mansion than if it had been in Chancery; not even the old woman in a bonnet—not even a baker's barrow delivering the daily loaf—not so much as a postman. He might almost have beguiled himself into the belief that the whole experience of that

November evening—the old man—the pale poetic-looking girl—the marvellous collection of art treasures seen by the flickering light of a single candle—were the mere phantasmagoria of an overworked brain, a waking dream, the inchoate vision of a disordered fancy.

He went twice every Sunday to a church that stood midway between his own house and the once regal mansion; a new church of the Pugin-Gothic order, with open seats, a painted window, other windows which awaited the piety of the congregation to be also painted, and a very young incumbent of the advanced type, deeply read in the lives of the saints, and given to early services. This temple was so small that Lucius fancied he could scarcely have failed to see Miss Sivewright were she a worshipper there. Sunday after Sunday, during the hymns, ancient and modern, he looked with anxious gaze round the fane, hoping to see that one interesting face among the crowd of uninteresting faces. Four out of five of the congregation were women, but Lucille Sivewright was not one of them. He began to resign himself to the dreary truth that they two were doomed never to meet again.

Hope, in its last agony, was suddenly recalled to new life. He came home from his daily drudgery one evening, thoroughly tired, even a little disheartened; 'discouraged,' as the American lady described herself, when she confessed to poisoning eight of her relations, simply because she began to regard them as encumbrances, and feared that, if permitted to live, they might reduce her to poverty. On this particular evening the star of science—that grand and ever-sustaining idea that he was to sow the seed of some new truth in the broad field of scientific progress—waxed paler than usual, and Lucius also was discouraged. He came home bodily and mentally tired. He had been tramping to and fro all day under a drizzling rain, and in a leaden atmosphere laden with London smoke.

Even in that shabby ill-built domicile which he called home, sorry comfort awaited him. His ancient serving-woman, Mrs. Babb, had let the parlour fire go out. The kettle, which, singing on the hob above a cheerful blaze, seemed almost a sentient thing, now leaned on one side disconsolately against a craggy heap of black coal, like a vessel aground upon a coral reef. The tray of tea-things—the neat white cloth indicative of chop or steak—adorned not his small round table. Mrs. Babb, absorbed in the feminine delights of a weekly cleaning, had suffered herself to become unconscious of the lapse of time.

He gave the loose, ill-hung bell-wire an angry jerk, flung himself into his accustomed arm-chair, and stretched out his hand haphazard in search of a book. Plato, Montaigne, Sterne, any philosopher who should teach him how to bear the petty stings of the scorpion—daily life.

But before his hand touched the volumes, its motion was arrested. He beheld something more interesting than Plato, since in all probability it concerned himself, namely, a letter, at a corner of the mantelpiece, just on a level with his eye. Egotism triumphed over philosophy. The letter, were it even a bill, was more vital to him for the moment than all the wisdom of Socrates.

He snatched the envelope, which was directed in a rugged uncompromising caligraphy, unfamiliar to him. He tore it open eagerly, and looked at the signature, 'Homer Sivewright.'

'Dear Sir,—When you obliged me with your assistance the other day, I believe I made some profane remark about your profession, which you took in good part. One forgives such gibes from a testy old man. You told me that when I found myself ill, my thoughts would naturally tend towards Savile-row. There you were wrong. I do find something out of gear in my constitution—possibly liver—or perhaps general break-up. But instead of thinking of the high-flyers of the West-end, with their big fees and pompous pretensions, I think of you.

'I told you the other night that I liked your face. This is not all. My housekeeper, who has kindred in this district, informs me that you have worked some marvellous cure upon her husband's brother's second cousin's wife's sister. The relationship is remote, but the rumour of your skill has reached my servant. Will you come this way at your convenience? Don't come out of your way on purpose to see me. My means, as I informed you, and as you might see for yourself in all my surroundings, are scanty, and I can afford to pay very little more than the poorest among your patients. I state the case thus plainly that there may be no future disagreement.—Truly yours,

'Homer Sivewright.'

'Is the old man a miser; or an enthusiast, who has sacrificed himself and his granddaughter to his love of art? Equally hard upon the granddaughter in either case,' reflected Lucius, trying to contemplate the business in the chilly light of common sense, wondering at and half-ashamed of the sudden delight which had moved him when he found that Mr. Sivewright's letter was nothing less than a passport to Lucille Sivewright's home.

'I'll go the instant I've dined,' he said to himself, giving another tug at the loose bell-wire. 'Yet who knows whether the old churl will let me see his interesting granddaughter? Perhaps he'll put me on a strictly professional footing; have me shown up to his den by that old woman, and shown down again without so much as a glimpse of Lucille's pensive face. Yet he can hardly pay me badly and treat me badly too. I'll ask permission to attend him as a friend; and then perhaps he'll melt a little, and admit me to his hearth. I like the look of that old wainscoted room, with its bare floor and clean-swept hearth, and handful of bright fire. It seemed to breathe the poetry of poverty.'

Mrs. Babb came clattering in with the tea-things and chop all together, profuse in apologies for having forgotten to wind up the kitchen clock, and thus become oblivious as to time.

'On a clear day I can see the clock at the public round the corner by stretching my head out of the back-attic window,' she said; 'but being thick to-day I couldn't, and I must have been an hour behind ever since dinner. And the fire gone out too!'

The fire was quickly lighted; the kettle carried off to boil down-stairs; but Lucius didn't wait for his tea. That gentle decoction, which was, in a general way, the very support of his life, to-night was almost indifferent to him. He ate his chop, ran up to his narrow dressing-room, where the weekly cleansing process had left a healthy odour of mottled soap and a refreshing dampness, washed away the smoke and grime of the day with much cold water, changed all his garments, lest he should carry the taint of fever-dens whither he was going, and went forth as gaily as to a festival.

'Am I as great a fool as dear old Geoffrey?' he asked himself during that rapid walk. 'No; at least I know something of my goddess. I could read the story of her patient self-sacrificing life even in that one hour. Besides, I am by no means in love with her. I am only interested.'

It was a new feeling for him to approach the gate with the certainty of admission. He tugged resolutely at the iron ring, and heard the rusty wires creak their objection to such disturbance. Then came a shuffling slipshod step across the barren forecourt, which, with different tenants, might have been a garden. This footstep announced the old woman in the bonnet, who seemed to him the twin sister of his own housekeeper, so closely do old women in that sphere of life resemble each other—like babies. She mumbled something, and admitted him to the sacred precincts. The same half-light glimmered in the hall as when he had seen it first; the whole treasury of art wrapped in shadow. The same brighter glow streamed from the panelled parlour as the old woman opened the door and announced 'Dr. Davory.' Homer Sivewright was sitting in his high-backed arm-chair by the hearth, getting all the heat he could out of the contracted fire. His granddaughter sat opposite him, knitting with four needles, which flashed like electric wires under the guidance of the soft white hands. The tea-tray—with its quaint old teapot in buff and black Wedgewood—adorned the table.

'I thought you'd come,' said the old man, 'though my letter was not very inviting, if you cultivate wealthy patients.'

'I do not,' answered Lucius, taking the chair indicated to him, after receiving a stately foreign curtsy from Miss Sivewright, an unfamiliar recognition which seemed to place him at an ineffable distance. 'I was very glad to get your note, and to respond to it promptly. I shall be still more glad if you will place my medical services upon a friendly footing. At your age a man requires the constant attendance of a doctor who knows his constitution. There may be very little treatment wanted, only the supervision of an experienced eye. Let me be your friend as well as your medical adviser, and drop in whenever I am wanted, without question of payment.'

The old man shot a keen glance from his cold gray eyes; eyes which looked as if they had been in the habit of prying into men's thoughts. 'Why should you be so generous?' he asked; 'I have no claim upon you, not even that hollow pretence which the world calls friendship. You have nothing to gain from me. My will, disposing of my collection—which is all I have to bequeath—was made ten years ago; and nothing would ever tempt me to alter it by so much as a ten-pound legacy. You see there's nothing to be gained by showing me kindness.'

'Grandfather!' remonstrated the girl, in her low serious voice.

'I am sorry you should impute to me any such sordid motive,' said Lucius quietly. 'My reason for offering my services gratis is plain and above board. There is no fireside at this end of the town at which I care to sit, no society congenial to me. I spend all my evenings alone, generally in hard study, sometimes with the books I love, or with my violin for my companion. This kind of life suits me well enough on the whole. Yet there are intervals of depression in which I feel its exceeding loneliness. No man is all-sufficient to himself. Give me the privilege of spending an evening here now and then—I will not wear out my welcome—and let me watch your case as a labour of love. You say that the recompense you can offer me will be small. Better for both your dignity and mine that there should be none at all.'

'You speak fair,' answered Sivewright, 'but that's a common qualification. I have a granddaughter there whom you may imagine to be my heiress. If she is, she is heiress only to my collection; and even my judgment may be mistaken as to the value of that. In any case, consider her disposed of—put her out of the question.'

'Grandfather!' remonstrated the girl again, this time blushing indignantly.

'Better to speak plainly, Lucille.'

'Since you cannot see me in any character except that of a fortune-hunter, sir,' said Lucius, rising, 'we had better put an end to the discussion. There are plenty of medical men in this neighbourhood. You can find an adviser among them. I wish you good-evening.'

'Stop,' exclaimed Sivewright, as the surgeon

walked straight to the door, wounded inexpressibly, 'I didn't mean to offend you. But you offered me your friendship, and it was best you should know upon what footing I could accept the offer. You now know that I have no money to leave any one—don't suppose me a miser because I live poorly; that's a common error—and that my granddaughter is disposed of. Knowing this, do you still offer me your professional services for nothing? do you still wish for a place beside my hearth?'

'I do,' said the young man eagerly, and with one swift involuntary glance at Lucille, who sat motionless, except for the dexterous hands that plied those shining wires. He thought of the humiliation of Hercules, and how well it would have pleased him to sit at her feet and hold the worsted that she wound.

'So be it then; you are henceforth free of this house. My door, which so seldom opens to a stranger, shall offer no barrier to you. If you discover circumstances in our lives that puzzle you, do not trouble yourself to wonder about them. You will know all in good time. Be a brother to Lucille.' She held out her hand to the visitor frankly at these words. He took it far more shyly than it was given. 'And be a son,' with a long regretful sigh, 'if you can, to me. I told you the other day that I liked your voice, that I liked your face. I will go farther to-night and say, I like you.'

'Thank you,' answered Lucius gravely, 'that is just what I want. I doubt if I have a near relation in the world, and I know but one man whom I count my friend. Friendship with me, therefore, means something very real. It is not a hackneyed sentiment, worn threadbare by long usage. But now that we have arranged things pleasantly, let us have our medical inspection.'

'Not to-night,' said Mr. Sivewright. 'Come to me to-morrow, if you can spare me the time. My symptoms are not of a pressing kind. I only feel the wheels of life somewhat clogged; the mainspring weaker than it used to be. Let us give to-night to friendship.'

'Willingly,' answered Lucius. 'I will be with you at ten o'clock to-morrow morning.'

He drew his chair nearer to the hearth, feeling that he was now really admitted to the charmed circle. To most young men it would have been far from an attractive house; for him it possessed an almost mysterious fascination. Indeed, it was perhaps the element of mystery which made Lucille Sivewright so interesting in his eyes. He had seen plenty of women who were as pretty—some who were more beautiful—but not one who had ever filled his thoughts as she did.

'Pour out the tea, child,' said Mr. Sivewright, and that fragrant beverage was dispensed by Lucille's white hands. It was one of the few details of housekeeping in which the old man permitted extravagance. The tea was of the choicest, brewed without stint, and the small antique silver jug, adorned with elaborate *repoussé* work, contained cream. Lucius thought he had never tasted anything so exquisite as that cup of tea. They sat round the fire, and the old man talked well and freely—talked of the struggles of his youth, his art-worship, those wonderful strokes of fortune to which the dealer in bric-à-brac is ever liable—talked of everything connected with his career, except his domestic life. On that one subject he was dumb.

Lucius thought of the castaway, the son who was of no more account to his father than one of the wooden images in the crowded storehouse across the hall. What had been his crime? Perhaps never to have been loved at all. This old man's nature seemed of a hard-grained wood, which could scarcely put forth tender shoots and blossoms of affection—a man who would consider his son his natural enemy.

'You spoke of your violin some time ago,' Lucille

said, by and by, in a pause of the conversation. Mr. Sivewright, having talked about himself to his heart's content, leaned back in his chair and contemplated the fire. 'Do you really play? I am so fond of the violin.'

'Are you, indeed?' cried Lucius, enraptured. 'I'll bring it some night, and—'

'Don't!' ejaculated the old man decisively. 'I am something of Chesterfield's opinion, that fiddling is beneath a gentleman. If I hear you scraping catgut I shall lose all confidence in your medicines.'

'Then you shall not hear me,' said Lucius, with perfect good humour. He was determined to make friends with this grim old bric-à-brac dealer if he could, just as one resolves to overcome the prejudices of an unfriendly dog, believing that beneath his superficial savagery there must be a substratum of nobility. 'I only thought a little quiet music might amuse Miss Sivewright, since she says she is fond of the violin.'

'She doesn't know what she is fond of,' replied Sivewright testily; 'she is full of fancies and whims, and likes everything that I abhor. There, no tears, child,' as those dark gentle eyes filled; 'you know I hate those most of all.'

Lucius came to the rescue, and began to talk with

renewed vivacity, thus covering Lucille's confusion. He spoke of himself, giving all those details of his childhood and youth, the knowledge of which between new acquaintances at once establishes the familiarity that is half-way towards friendship.

He left early, fearful of outstaying his welcome; left with a sense of perfect content in this quiet domestic evening, although the old man had certainly not gone out of his way to conciliate his visitor. Lucille had talked very little, but even her silence had been interesting to Lucius. It seemed to him the indication, not of dulness, but of a gentle melancholy; a mind overshadowed by some olden sorrow, and perhaps depressed by the solitude of that dreary mansion. He was not satisfied with a continental curtsy at parting, but offered Lucille his hand, which she took as frankly as if she had fully accepted him in the character of an adopted brother.

CHAPTER V.

'I HAD A SON, NOW OUTLAW'D FROM MY BLOOD.'

TEN o'clock the next morning beheld Lucius again at the tall gate. He was admitted without question, and the open door of the parlour showed him Lucille—in a gray stuff gown, a large linen apron, and a white muslin cap, like a French grisette's—rubbing the oaken wainscot with a beeswaxed cloth; while a small tub of water on the table and some china cups and saucers set out to drain, showed that she had been washing the breakfast things. This circumstance explained the spotless neatness of all he had seen— the shining wainscot, the absence of a grain of dust upon any object in the room. She came out to wish him good-morning, nowise abashed.

'I daresay your English young ladies would think this very shocking,' she said. 'I ought to be practising Czerny's *Exercises de Facilité*, ought I not, at this time in the morning?'

'Our English girls are very stupid when they devote all their time to Czerny,' he answered, ' to the utter disregard of their domestic surroundings. I'm not going to talk that hackneyed trash which Cobbett brought into fashion, about preferring the art of making puddings to music and literature; but I think it simply natural to a woman of refinement to superintend the arrangements of her home—yes, and to use brooms and dusters, rather than allow resting-place for so much as a drachm of flue or dust. But you talk of our English ladies as a race apart. Are you not English, Miss Sivewright?'

'Only on my father's side, and his mother was a Spanish-American. My mother' (with a sigh) ' was a Frenchwoman.'

'Ah,' thought Lucius, 'it is in such mixed races one finds beauty and genius.'

How pretty she looked in her little muslin cap, adorning but not concealing the rich dark hair! How well the neutral-tinted gown, with its antique simplicity, became her graceful form!

'Talking of music,' he said, ' have you no piano ?'

'No, I am sorry to say. My grandfather has a prejudice against music.'

'Indeed! There are few who care to confess such a singular prejudice.'

'Perhaps it is because'—falteringly and trifling nervously with the linen band of her apron—' because a person with whom he quarrelled long ago was fond of music.'

'A somewhat unreasonable reason. And you are thus deprived of even such companionship as you might find in a piano! That seems hard.'

'Pray do not blame my grandfather: he is very good to me. I have an old guitar—my mother's—with which I amuse myself sometimes in my own room, where he can't hear me. Shall I show you the way to my grandfather's bedroom? He seldom comes down-stairs till after twelve o'clock.'

Lucius followed her up the broad oak staircase, which at each spacious landing was encumbered with specimens of those ponderous Flemish cabinets and buffets, which would seem to have sprung into being spontaneous as toadstools from the fertile soil of the Low Countries. Then along a dusky corridor, where ancient tapestry and dingy pictures covered the walls, to a door at the extreme end, which she opened.

'This is grandpapa's room,' she said, upon the threshold, and there left him.

He knocked at the half-open door, not caring to enter the lion's den unauthorised. A stern voice bade him 'Come in.'

The room was large and lofty, but so crowded with the same species of lumber as that which he had seen below that there was little more than a passage, or strait, whereby he could approach his patient. Here, too, were cabinets of ebony inlaid with *pietra dura;* in one corner stood an Egyptian mummy—perchance a departed Pharaoh, whose guilt-burdened soul had shivered at the bar of Osiris six thousand years ago; while on the wall above him hung a grim picture—of the early German school—representing the flaying of a saint and martyr, hideously faithful to anatomy. The opposite wall was entirely covered by moth-eaten tapestry, upon which the fair fingers of mediæval chatelaines had depicted the Dance of Death. Gazing with wondering eyes round the room, Lucius beheld elaborately-carved arm-chairs in Bombay black wood, peacock mosquito-fans, sandal-wood caskets, poonah work, and ivory chessmen; lamps that had lighted Roman catacombs or burned on Pagan altars; Highland quaichs from which Charles Edward may have drunk the native usquebaugh; a Greek shield, of the time of Alexander, shaped like the back of a tortoise; a Chinese idol; a South Sea islander's canoe. A hundred memories of lands remote, of ages lost in the midst of time, were suggested by this heterogeneous mass of property, which to the inexperienced eye of Lucius seemed more interesting than valuable.

The old man's bed stood in a corner near the fire-place—a small four-poster, with clumsily-carved columns, somewhat resembling that bedstead which the student of history gazes upon with awe in Mary Stuart's bedchamber at Holyrood, thinking how often that fair head must have laid itself down there, weary of cark and care, and crown and royal robes, and false friends and falser lovers—a shabby antique bedstead, with ragged hangings of faded red silk.

There was a fire in the grate, pinched like the grate below; a three-cornered chair of massive carved ebony, covered with stamped and gilded leather, stood beside it. Here sat the master of these various treasures, his long gray hair crowned with a black-velvet skullcap; his gaunt figure wrapped in a ragged damask dressing-gown, edged with well-worn fur; a garment which may have been coeval with the bedstead.

'Good-morning,' said Mr. Sivewright, looking up from his newspaper. 'You look surprised at the furniture of my bedroom; not room enough to swing a cat, is there? But you see I don't want to swing cats. When I get a bargain I bring it in here, and have it about me till I get tired of looking at it, and then Wincher and I carry it down-stairs to the general collection.'

'Wincher?'

'Yes, Jacob Wincher, my old Jack-of-all-trades; you haven't seen him yet? He burrows somewhere in the back premises—sleeps in the coal-cellar, I believe—and is about as fond of daylight and fresh air as a mole. A faithful fellow enough. He was my clerk and general assistant in Bond-street; here he amuses himself pottering about among my purchases; catalogues them after his own fashion, and could give a better statement of my affairs than any City accountant.'

'A valuable servant,' said Lucius.

'Do you think so? I haven't paid him anything for the last seven years. He stays with me, partly because he likes me in his slavish canine way, partly because he has nowhere else to go. His wife keeps my house, and takes care of Lucille. And now for our consultation; the pain in my side has been a trifle worse this morning.'

Lucius began his interrogatory. Gently, and with that friendly persuasiveness which had made him beloved by his parish patients, he drew from the old man a full confession of his symptoms. The case was grave. An existence joyless, hard, laborious, monotonous to weariness, will sometimes exhaust the forces of the body, sap the vital power, as perniciously as the wear and tear of riotous living. High pressure has pretty much the same effect, let the motive power be love of gain or love of pleasure. In a word, Homer Sivewright had worn himself out. There was chronic disease of long standing; there was general derangement which might end fatally sooner or later. He was over sixty years of age. He might die within the year; he might live two, three, four, five years longer.

'You have not spared yourself, I fear,' said Lucius, as he put his stethoscope into his pocket.

'No; I have always had one great object in life. A man who has that rarely spares himself.'

'Yet a man who wears himself out before his time by reckless labour is hardly wiser than those foolish virgins who left their lamps without oil.'

'Perhaps. It is not always easy to be wise. A man whose domestic life is a disappointment is apt to concentrate his labour and his thoughts upon some object outside his home. My youth was a hard one from necessity, my middle age was hard from habit. I had not acquired the habit of luxury. My trade grew daily more interesting to me, ten times more so than anything the world calls pleasure. I spent my days in sale-rooms, or wandering in those strange nooks and corners to which art treasures sometimes drift—the mere jetsam and flotsam of life's troubled

VOL. I. N

sea, the unconsidered spoil of ruined homes. My nights were devoted to the study of my ledger, or the text-books of my trade. I had no desire for any other form of life. If I could have afforded all the comforts and pleasures of modern civilisation—which of course I could not—my choice would have kept me exactly where I was.'

'In future,' said Lucius in his cheery tone—he never discouraged a patient—' it will be well for you to live more luxuriously. Stint yourself in nothing, and let the money you have hitherto spent in adding to your collection be henceforth devoted to good old port and a liberal dietary.'

'I have spent nothing lately,' said Sivewright sharply; 'I have had nothing to spend.'

'I don't want to doubt your word,' replied Lucius; 'but I tell you frankly you must live better than you have done, if you wish to live much longer.'

'I do,' cried the old man with sudden energy; 'I have prayed for long life—I who pray so little. Yes, I have sent up that one supplication to the blind blank sky. I want to live for long years to come. If I had been born three hundred years ago, I should have sought for the sublime secret—the elixir of life. But I live in an age when men believe in nothing,' with a profound sigh.

'Say rather in an age when men reserve their faith for the God who made them, instead of exhausting their powers of belief upon crucibles and alembics,' answered Lucius in his most practical tone.

Then followed his *régime*, simple and sagacious, but to be followed strictly.

'I should like to say a few words to your granddaughter,' he said; 'so much in these cases depends upon good nursing.'

'Say what you please,' replied Mr. Sivewright, ringing his bell, 'but let it be said in my hearing. I don't relish the notion of being treated like a child; of having powders given me unawares in jam, or senna in my tea. If you have a sentence of death to pronounce, pronounce it fearlessly. I am stoic enough to hear my death-warrant unmoved.'

'I shall make no such demand upon your stoicism. The duration of your life will depend very much on your own prudence. Of course at sixty the avenue at the end of which a man sees his grave is not an endless perspective. But you have a comfortable time before you yet, Mr. Sivewright, if you will live wisely and make the most of it.'

Lucille came in response to the bell, and to her Lucius repeated his directions as to diet and general treatment.

'I am not going to dose your grandfather with drugs,' he said; 'a mild tonic, to promote appetite, is all I shall give him. He complains of sleeplessness, a natural effect of thinking much, and monotonously brooding on some one theme, and that not a pleasant one.'

The old man looked at him sharply, angrily even.

'I don't want any fortune-telling,' he said; 'stick to your text. You profess to cure the body, and not the mind.'

'Unless the mind will consent to assist the cure, my art is hopeless,' answered Lucius.

He finished his advice, dwelling much on that essential point, a generous diet. The girl looked at her grandfather doubtfully. He seemed to answer the look.

'The money must be found, child,' he said, in a fretful tone, 'if I part with the gems of my collection. After all, life is the great necessity; all ends with that.'

'You will find your spare cash better bestowed upon your own requirements than on Egyptian mummies,' said Lucius, with a disparaging glance at the defunct Pharaoh.

Mr. Sivewright promised to be guided by his counsel, and civilly dismissed him.

'Come to me as often as you like,' he said, 'since

you come as a friend; and let it be in the evening if that is pleasantest to you. I suppose there will be no necessity for any more serious examinations like this morning's,' with a faint smile, and a disagreeable recollection of the stethoscope, which instrument seemed to him as much an emblem of death as the skull and crossbones on an old tombstone.

Lucius and Lucille went down-stairs together, and he lingered a little in the oak-panelled parlour, from which all tokens of her housewifery cares had now vanished. A bunch of violets and snowdrops in a tall Venetian beaker stood in the centre of the table; a few books, an open workbasket, indicated the damsel's morning occupation. She had taken off her linen apron, but not the cap, which gave the faintest spice of coquetry to her appearance, and which Lucius thought the prettiest headgear he had ever seen.

They talked a little of the old man up-stairs; but the surgeon was careful not to alarm Mr. Sivewright's granddaughter. Alas, poor child, coldly and grudgingly as he acknowledged her claim upon him, he was her only guardian, the sole barrier between her and the still colder world outside her gloomy home.

'You do not think him *very* ill?' she asked anxiously.

'I do not think there is any reason for you to be anxious. Careful I am sure you will be; and care may do much to prolong his life. He has used himself hardly.'

'Yes,' she answered in a mournful tone. 'He has had troubles, heavy troubles, and he broods upon them.'

'Change of air and scene might be advantageous. There is an oppressive atmosphere in such a house as this, in such a quarter of the town.'

'I have sometimes found it so.'

'When the spring comes, say about the middle of April, I should strongly recommend a change for you both. To Hastings, for instance.'

The girl shook her head despondently.

'He would never consent to spend so much money,' she said. 'We are very poor.'

'Yet Mr. Sivewright can find money for his purchases.'

'They cost so little; a few shillings at a time. The things he buys are bargains, which he discovers in strange out-of-the-way places.'

'Is he often out of doors?'

'Yes, and for long hours together. But lately he has been more fatigued after those long rambles than he used to be.'

'He must abandon them altogether. And you have spent some years alone in this old house?'

'Yes. I am accustomed to solitude. It is rather dull sometimes. But I have my books, and the house to take care of, for old Mrs. Wincher does only the rougher part of the work, and some pleasant memories of the past to amuse me when I sit and think.'

'Is your past a very bright one?'

'Only the quiet life of a school in Yorkshire, where I was sent when I was very young, and where I stayed till I was seventeen. But the life seemed bright to me. I had governesses and schoolfellows whom I loved, and green hills and woods that were only less dear than my living friends.'

This paved the way for farther confidences. She spoke of her youth, he of his; of his father and mother, of his sister, the little one buried in the family grave, not that other whose fate he knew not; his college days; things he had spoken of the night before. She stopped him in the middle.

'Tell me about America,' she said; 'I want to know all about America. Some one I loved very much went to America.'

'I should have hardly thought your life had been eventful enough for much love,' said Lucius somewhat coldly.

'I have not seen the person I speak of since I was seven years old,' she answered, with a sigh. 'I think I may trust you; we are friends, are we not?'

'Did not your grandfather authorise me to consider myself almost your adopted brother?'

'The person I spoke of just now is one whose very name is forbidden here. But that cruelty cannot make me forget him. It only strengthens my memory. He is my father.'

'Your father? Yes, I understand; the son whom your grandfather cast off. But not without cause, I suppose?'

'Perhaps not,' answered Lucille, the dark deep eyes filling with tears that were quickly brushed away. 'He may have been to blame. My grandfather has never told me why they quarrelled. He has only told me in hard cruel words that they learned to hate each other before they learned to forget each other. I was not old enough to know anything except that my father was always kind to me, and always dear to me. I did not see him very much. He was out a great deal, out late at night, and I was alone with an old servant in my grandfather's house in Bond-street, where we had lived ever since I could remember, though I was not born there. We had a dark little parlour behind the shop, which went back a long way, and was crowded like the room on the other side of the hall. The days used to seem very long and dull, so little sunshine, so little air. But everything grew bright when papa came in for an hour, and took me on his knee, and told me long wild stories, German stories, I believe, yet half his own invention; stories of kelpies and lurleys and haunted castles, of a world that was peopled with fairies, where every leaf and every flower had its sprite. But I shall tire you with all this talk,' she said, checking herself suddenly; 'and perhaps your patients are waiting for you.'

'They must wait a few minutes longer. Tire me? no, I am deeply interested in all you tell me. Pray go on. Those were your happy hours which your father spent at home.'

'Happy beyond all measure. Sometimes, of a winter's evening—winter was the pleasantest time in that dark little parlour—he would sit idly by the fire in a great arm-chair; sometimes he would take his violin from a shelf in the corner by the chimney-piece, and play to me. I used to climb upon his knee, and sit half buried in the big chair while he played; such sweet music, low and solemn, like the music of one's dreams. I have heard nothing like it since. Those were happy nights when he stayed at home till I went to bed, happy hours beside the fire. We used to have no light in the room but the fire-light, and I fancied the shadowy corners were full of fairies.'

'Did you hear nothing of the quarrel between your father and your grandfather? Children, even at seven years old, are quick to observe.'

'No. If they quarrelled it was not in my hearing. My grandfather lived entirely in his business. He seldom came into the parlour except for his meals, or until late at night, when I had gone to bed. I only know that one morning he was very ill, and when he came down-stairs he had an awful look in his face, like the face of a man risen from the grave, and he beckoned me to him, and told me my father had gone away, for ever. I cannot tell you my grief, it was almost desperate. I wanted to run away, to follow my father. And one night, which I remember, O so well, a wet winter night, I got up and put on my clothes somehow, after Mrs. Wincher had put me to bed, and crept down the dark staircase, and opened the door in the passage at the side of the shop, which was rarely used, and went out into the wet streets. I can see the lamps reflected on the shining pavement to this day, if I shut my eyes, and feel the cold wet wind blowing upon my face.'

'Poor child!'

'Yes, I was a very miserable child that night. I wandered about for a long time, looking for my father in the crowd; sometimes following a figure that looked like his ever so far, only to find I had followed a stranger. I remember the shop windows being shut one by one, and the streets growing dark and empty, and how at last I grew frightened, and sat down on a doorstep and began to cry. A policeman came across the street and looked at me, and shook me roughly by the arm, and then began to question me. I was quite disheartened by this time, and had given up all hope of finding my father: so I told him my name and where I lived, and he took me home, through a great many narrow streets and turnings and windings. I must have walked a long way, for I know I had crossed one of the bridges over the river. Everybody had gone to bed when the policeman knocked at the door in Bond-street. My flight had not been found out. My grandfather came down to open the door in his dressing-gown and slippers. He didn't even scold me, he seemed too much surprised for that, when he saw me wet and muddy and footsore. He gave the man money, and carried me up to my little bed-room at the top of the house, and lighted a fire with his own hands, and did all he could to make me warm and comfortable. He asked me why I had gone out, and I told him. Then for the first time that I can remember, he took me in his arms and kissed me. "Poor Luce," he said, "poor little orphan girl!" He was very kind to me for the next three days, and then took me down to Yorkshire to the school, where I stayed nearly ten years.'

'A strange sad story,' said Lucius, deeply interested. 'And have you never been told your father's fate?'

'Only that he went to America, and that my grandfather has never heard of him from the hour in which they parted until now.'

'May he not have had some tidings, and kept the truth from you?'

'I don't think he would tell me a direct falsehood; and he has most positively declared that he has received no letter from my father, and has heard nothing of him from any other source. He is dead, no doubt. I cannot think that he would quite forget the little girl who used to sit upon his knee.'

'You believe him to have been a good father then, in spite of your grandfather's condemnation of him?'

'I believed that he loved me.'

'Have you no recollection of your mother?'

'No. She must have died when I was very

young. I have seen her portrait. My grandfather keeps it hidden away in his desk, with old letters, and other relics of the past. I begged him once to give it to me, but he refused. "Better forget that you ever had a father or a mother," he said, in his bitterest tone. But I have not forgotten my mother's face, and its sweet thoughtful beauty.'

'I am ready to believe that she was beautiful,' said Lucius, with a tender smile. Lucille's story had brought them ever so much nearer together. Now, indeed, he might allow himself to be interested in her—might freely surrender himself captive to the charm of her gentle beauty—the magic of her sympathetic voice. That little pathetic picture of her sorrowful childhood—a tender heart overflowing with love that none cared to garner—*that* made him her slave for ever. Was this love at first sight, that foolish unreasoning passion, which in Geoffrey Hossack he deemed akin to lunacy? No, rather an intuitive recognition of the one woman in all the world created to be the sharer of his brightest hopes, the object of his sweetest solicitude, the recompense and crown of his life. He had to tear himself away after only a few friendly words, for Duty, speaking with the voice of his parish patients, seemed to call him from this enchanted scene.

'I shall look in once or twice a week, in the evening,' he said, 'and keep a watchful eye upon my patient. Good-bye.'

Towards the end of that week he spent another evening at Cedar House, and in the following week two more evenings and so on, through windy March, and in the lengthening days of April, until he looked back and wondered how he had managed to live before his common-place existence had been brightened by these glimpses of a fairer world. The old man grew still more familiar—friendly even—and allowed the two young people to talk at their ease; nor did he seem to have any objection to their growing intimacy. As the days grew longer, he suffered them to wander about the old house in the spring twilight, and out into a desert in the rear, which had once been a garden, where there still remained an ancient cedar, with skeleton limbs that took grim shapes in the dusk. Not a second Eden, by any means, for this blossomless garden ended in a creek, where grimy barges, laden with rubble or sand, or rags, or bones, or coal, or old iron, lay lopsided in the inky mud, against the mouldering woodwork of a dilapidated wharf, waiting to be disburdened of their freight.

Yet to one at least these wanderings, these lingering *tête-à-têtes* by the creek, looking down dreamily at the Betsy Jane of Wapping, or the Ann Smith of Bermondsey, were all-sufficient for happiness.

Seeing the old man thus indulgent, Lucius assured himself that he could have formed no other views about his granddaughter; since, as Lucius himself thought, it would naturally occur to him that he, Lucius, must needs fall madly in love with her. He felt all the more secure upon this point since he had so long been a constant visitor at Cedar House, and had met no one there who could pretend to Miss Sivewright's favour. A snuffy old dealer had been once or twice closeted with Mr. Sivewright, but that was all. And however base a tyrant Lucille's grandfather might be, he could scarcely contemplate bestowing his lovely grandchild upon an old man in a shabby coat, who presented himself on the threshold of the parlour with an abject air, and brought some object of art or virtu wrapped in a blue-cotton handkerchief for the connoisseur's inspection.

So the year grew older, and Lucius Davoren looked out upon a new existence, cheered by new hopes, and happy thoughts which went with him through the long days of toil, and whispered to his soul in the pauses of his studious nights.

Even the hideous memory of what went before his illness in America—that night in the pine-forest, that winter dusk when the wicked face looked in at his window, when the wolfish eyes glared at him for the last time, save in his dreams—even that dread picture faded somewhat, and he could venture to meditate calmly upon the details of that tragedy, and say to himself, 'The blood I shed yonder was justly shed.'

CHAPTER VI.

'BY HEAVEN, I LOVE THEE BETTER THAN MYSELF.'

WHILE Lucius dreamed his dream beside the wharf where the barges lay moored under the smoky London sky, Geoffrey was following his siren from one provincial town to another, not without some enjoyment in the chase, which filled his empty life with some kind of object, no matter though it were a foolish one. Given youth, health, activity, and a handsome income, there yet remains something wanting to a man's existence, without which it is apt to become more or less a burden to him. That something is a purpose. Geoffrey having failed—from very easiness of temper, from being everybody's favourite, first in every pleasure-party, foremost in every sport that needed pluck and endurance, rather than from lack of ability—to achieve distinction at the University, had concluded that he was fit for nothing particular in life; that he had no vocation, no capacity for distinguishing himself from the ruck of his fellow men; and that the best thing he could do was to live upon the ample fortune his merchant father had amassed for him, and get as much pleasure as he could out of life.

Almost his first experience of pleasure and independence had been those two years' travel in the Far West. Pleasure in that particular instance had brought him face to face with death, but was counted pleasure nevertheless. After doing America, he had done as much of the old world as he happened to feel interested in doing, not scampering round the globe in ninety days like Mr. Cook's excursionists, but taking an autumn in Norway, a winter in Rome, a spring in Greece, a summer in Sweden, and so on, until he began to feel, in his own colloquial phrase, that he had used up the map of Europe.

Apart from his passion for the lovely concert-singer, Mrs. Bertram, which was strong enough to have sustained his energies had the siren sought to lure him to the summit of Mount Everest, he really enjoyed this scamper from one provincial town to another, these idle days spent in sleepy old cities, which were as new to him as any unexplored region in central Europe. The great dusky cathedrals or abbey-churches into which he strolled before breakfast, careless but not irreverent, and where he sometimes found white-robed curates and choristers chanting the matin service; the empty square, where the town-pump and a mediæval cross had it all to themselves, except on market-days; the broad turnpike-road beyond the High-street, where, perhaps, an avenue of elms on the outskirt of the town testified to the beneficent care of some bygone corporation not quite destitute of a regard for the picturesque; these things, which repeated themselves, with but little variety, in most of the towns he explored, were not without a certain mild interest for Mr. Hossack.

He would gaze in wondering contemplation upon those handsome red-brick houses at the best end of the High-street, those respectable middle-class houses which every one knows, and of which every English town can boast, no matter how remote from the fever of that commerce which makes the wealth of nations. Houses whose windows shine resplendent, without stain or blemish of dust, smoke, or weather; houses on whose spotless doorstep no foot seems to have trodden, whose green balconies are filled with geraniums more scarlet than other geraniums, and on whose stems no faded leaf appears; houses whose sacred interior—archtemple of those homelier British virtues, ready money and soapsuds—is shrouded from the vulgar eye by starched muslin curtains pendant from brazen rods; houses at which the taxgatherer never calls twice, doors whose shining knockers have never trembled in the rude grasp of a dun.

Sometimes, in the gloaming, Geoffrey beheld the bald head of an elderly gentleman above the brass curtain-rod, and a pair of elderly eyes gazing gravely across the empty street, not as if they expected to see anything. The brass plate on the door would inform him of the elderly gentleman's profession— whether he was family solicitor or family surgeon, architect or banker; and then Mr. Hossack would lose himself in a labyrinth of wonder, marvelling how this old man had borne the burden of his days in that atmosphere of monotonous respectability, always looking out of the same shining window, above the same brazen bar. He would go back to his hotel, after this small study of human life, a wiser and a happier man, thanking Providence for that agreeable combination of youth, health, and independent fortune which gave him, in a manner, the key of the universe.

Stillmington, in Warwickshire, was a place considerably in advance of the dull old market towns where one could hear the butcher's morning salutation to his neighbour from one end of the street to the other, where, indeed, the buzzing of a lively bluebottle made an agreeable interruption of the universal silence. Stillmington lay in the bosom of a fine hunting country, and, as long as foxes were in season, was gay with the cheery clatter of horses' hoofs on its well-kept roads, the musical clink of spurs on its spotless pavements. Stillmington boasted an aristocractic hotel, none of your modern limited-liability palaces, but a family hotel of the fine old English expensive and exclusive school, where people ate and drank in the splendid solitude of their private apartments, and stared at one another superciliously when they met in the corridors or on the staircase, instead of herding together at stated intervals to gorge themselves in the eye of their fellow man, like the passengers on board a Cunard steamer. Stillmington possessed also a wholesome spring, whose health-restoring waters were, however, somewhat out of vogue, and a public garden, through whose leafy groves meandered that silvern but weedy stream the river Still; a garden whose beauties were somewhat neglected by the upper five hundred of Stillmington, except on the occasion of an archery meeting or a croquet tournament.

In the bright April weather, all sunshine and blue skies, like a foretaste of summer, Geoffrey found himself at Stillmington. His enchantress had been delighting the ruder inhabitants of Burleysbury, the great manufacturing town fifteen miles away, whose plethora of wealth served to sustain the expensive elegance of her unproductive neighbour, and was now at Stillmington. There were to be two concerts, with an interval of a week between them, and Geoffrey, whose knowledge of Mrs. Bertram's movements was of the fullest, had ascertained that she meant to spend that intervening week in Stillmington. He had followed her from town to town, through all the deviations of a most circuitous tour; now at Brighton, anon at Liverpool, now at Cheltenham, anon at York. He had heard her sing the same songs again and again, and had known no weariness. But in all his wanderings he had never yet spoken to her. It was not that he lacked boldness. He had written to her— letters enough to have made a bulky volume had he cared to publish those sentimental compositions— but on her part there had been only the sternest silence. No response whatever had been vouchsafed to those fervid epistles, offering his hand and fortune, his heart's best blood even, if she should happen to desire such a sacrifice; letters teeming with unconscious and somewhat garbled quotations from Byron, made eloquent by plagiarism from Moore, with here and there a touch of that energetic passion which glows in the love-songs of Robert Burns; yet to the very core honest and manly and straightforward and true. She must have been colder than ice surely to have been unmoved by such letters.

She had recognised the writer. That he knew. However crowded the hall where she sang, Geoffrey knew that his presence was not unperceived by her. He saw a swift sudden glance shot from those deep gray eyes as she curtsied her acknowledgment of the applause that welcomed her entrance; that keen glance which swept the crowd and rested for one ecstatic moment upon him. The lovely face never stirred from its almost statuesque repose—a pensive gravity, as of one who had done with the joys and emotions of life—yet he had fancied more than once that the eyes brightened as they recognised him; as if even to that calm spirit there were some sense of triumph in the idea of so much dogged devotion, such useless worship.

'I daresay she feels pretty much as Astarte, or Baal, or any of those ancient parties would have felt, if they had been capable of feeling, when they were propitiated with human sacrifices. She won't answer my letters, or afford me a ray of encouragement, but likes to know that there is an honest fool breaking his heart for her. No matter. I would rather break my heart for her than live happy ever afterwards, as the story-books say, with any one else. So courage, Geoffrey; let us show her how much ill-usage true lovers can bear, and still love on, and hope on, till love and hope are extinguished together in one untimely grave.'

And Geoffrey, whose philosophic mind was wont thus to relieve the tedium of the toilet, would contemplate his visage in the glass as he arranged his white tie, and wonder that ill-starred passion had not made greater ravages in his countenance; that he had not grown pale and wan, and seamed with premature wrinkles.

'I wonder I'm not as grim-looking as Count Ugolino, by this time,' he said to himself; and then went down to his private sitting-room at the Royal George, to eat a dinner of five courses in solitary state, for the benefit of that old-established family hotel. Love as yet had not affected his appetite. He did excellent justice to the *cuisine* of the *chef* at the George, an artist far above the common type of hotel cooks.

This young worldling was not without expedients. Inaccessible as his bright particular star might be, he yet contrived to scrape acquaintance with one of the lesser lights in that planetary system of which she was a part. A little finesse and a good deal of brandy-and-soda obtained for him the friendship of a youthful pianist, whose duty it was to accompany the singers. From this youth, who wore his hair long, affected the dreamily classical school, and believed himself a mute inglorious Chopin, Geoffrey heard all that was to be heard about Mrs. Bertram. But, alas, this all was little more than the musicsellers had already told him.

No one knew any more about her than the one fact of her supreme isolation, and that reserve of manner which was, perhaps unjustly, called pride. She lived alone; received no one, visited no one, kept her fellow performers at the farthest possible distance. If she took a lodging, it was always remote from the quarter affected by the rest of the little company; if she stayed at an hotel, it was never the hotel chosen by the others.

So much as this Geoffrey contrived to hear—not once only, but many times—without committing himself to the faintest expression of his feelings. He would have perished sooner than degrade his passion by making it the subject of vulgar gossip.

'If I cannot win her without a go-between,' he said to himself, 'I am not worthy of her.'

Many times, stung to the quick by the freezing

contempt with which she treated his letters, he had watched and lain in wait for her, determined to force an interview, should the opportunity arise. But no such opportunity had yet arisen. He would do nothing to create a scandal.

Here at Stillmington he had new hopes. The little town was almost empty, and offered a depressing prospect to the speculator who was to give the two concerts. The hunting season was over; the water-drinking and summer-holiday season had not yet begun. Stillmington had assumed its most exclusive aspect. The residents—a class who held themselves infinitely above those birds of passage who brought life and gaiety and a brisk circulation of ready money to the place—had it all to themselves. Respectable old Anglo-Indian colonels and majors paraded the sunny High-street, slow and solemn and gouty, and passed the time of day with their acquaintance on the opposite pavements in stentorian voices, which all the town might hear, and with as much confidence in the splendour of their social position as if they had been the ground-landlords of the town. Indeed, the lords of the soil were for the most part a very inferior race of men, who wore dusty coats, shabby hats with red-cotton handkerchiefs stuffed into the crown, and had a sprinkling of plaster of paris in their hair, and a three-foot rule sticking **out** of their breast pockets—men who belong to the bricklaying interest, and had **come into** Stillmington thirty years ago, footsore and penniless, in search of labour. These in their secret souls made light **of the** loud-voiced majors.

The town was very quiet; the glades and groves **in the** subscription garden—where the young lilacs put forth their tender leaves in the spring sunshine, and the first of the nightingales began her plaintive jug-jug at eventide—were lonely as those pathless regions of brushwood at the mouth of the Mississippi where the alligator riots at large among his scaly tribe. To this garden came Geoffrey, on the second day of his residence at Stillmington. Mr. Shinn, the pianist, had dropped a few words that morning, which were all-sufficient to make this one spot the most attractive in the world for Geoffrey Hossack. Mrs. Bertram and her little girl had walked here yesterday afternoon. Mr. Shinn **had seen them** go in at the gate while he was enjoying a meditative cigar, and **thinking** out a reverie in C minor during his after-dinner **stroll**.

Geoffrey was prompt to act upon this information. **What more** likely than that his divinity would walk in the same place this afternoon? There was a blue sky, and the west wind was balmy as midsummer zephyrs. All nature invited her to those verdant groves.

Mr. Hossack paid his money at the little gate, where a comfortable-looking gatekeeper was dozing over a local newspaper, and went in. Nature had liberally assisted the landscape gardener who laid out the Stillmington Eden. Geoffrey followed a path which wound gently through a shady grove, athwart whose undergrowth of rhododendron and laurel flashed the bright winding river. Here and there a break in the timber revealed a patch of green lawn sloping to the bank, where willows dipped their tremulous leafage into the rippling water. Ferns, and such pale flowers as will flourish in the shade —primrose, wild hyacinth, and periwinkle—grew luxuriantly upon the broken ground beside the path, where art had concealed itself beneath an appearance of wildness. To the right of this grove there was a wide stretch of lawn, where the toxophilites held their festivals—where the croquet balls went perpetually on certain days of the week, from the first of May to the last of September. But happily the croquet season had not yet begun, and the birds had grove and lawn to themselves.

Geoffrey went to the end of the grove, meeting

no one. He strolled down to the bank and looked at the river, contemplated the weeds with the eye of boatman and of angler.

'It ought to be a good place for jack,' he muttered, yawned, and went back to the grove.

It was lonely as before. Thrushes, linnets, blackbirds, burst forth with their little gushes of melody, now alone, now together, then lapsed into silence. He could hear the fish leap in the river; he could hear the faint splash of the willow branches shaken by the soft west wind. He yawned again, walked back to within a few yards of the gate, came back again, stretched himself, looked at his watch, and sank exhausted on a rustic seat under the leafy arm of a chestnut.

'I wonder if she will come to-day,' he thought, wishing he had been at liberty to solace himself with a cigar. 'It would be just like my luck if she didn't. If I had only seen her yesterday instead of that ass Shinn, with his confounded reverie in C minor. But there was I loafing at the other end of the town, expecting to find her looking at the shop windows, or getting a novel at the circulating library, when I ought to have been down here. And if I ever do contrive to speak to her, I wonder what she'll say. Treat me with contumely, no doubt; blight me with her scorn, as she has blighted my epistolary efforts. And yet, sometimes, I have seen a look in those gray eyes that seemed to say, "What, are you so true? Would to God I could reward your truth!" A delusion, of course—mad as my love for her.'

The mildness of the atmosphere, those little gushes of song from the birds, the booming buzz of an industrious bee, the faint ripple of the river, made a combination of sound that by and by beguiled him into forgetfulness, or not quite forgetfulness, rather a pleasant blending of waking thought and dreaming fancy. How long this respite from the cares of actual life lasted he knew not; but after a while the sweet voice of his enchantress, which had mingled itself with all his dreams, seemed to grow more distinct, ceased to be a vague murmur responsive to the voice of his heart, and sounded clear and ringing in the still afternoon atmosphere. He woke with a start, and saw a tall slim figure coming slowly along the path, half in sunshine, half in shadow—a lady with a face perfect as a Greek sculptor's Helen, dark chestnut hair, eyes of that deep gray which often seems black—a woman about whose beauty there could hardly be two opinions. She was dressed in black and gray—a black-silk dress of the simplest fashion, a loose mantle of some soft gray stuff, which draped her like a statue, a bonnet made of black lace and violets.

She was talking to a little girl with a small round face, which might or might not by and by develop into some likeness of the mother's beauty. The child carried a basket, and knelt down every now and then to gather primroses and violets on the uneven ground beside the path.

'Sweet child,' said Geoffrey within himself, apostrophising the infant, 'if you would only run ever so far away, and leave me quite free to talk to your mamma!'

He rose and went to meet her, taking off his hat as she approached.

'I would not lose such an opportunity for worlds,' he thought, 'even at the risk of being considered a despicable cad. I'll speak to her.'

She tried to pass him, those glorious eyes overlooking him with a superb indifference, not a sign of discomposure in her countenance. But he was resolute.

'Mrs. Bertram,' he began, 'pray pardon me for my audacity: desperation is apt to be rash. I have tried every means of obtaining an introduction to you, and am driven to this from very despair.'

She gave him a look which made him feel infinitely small in his own estimation.

'You have chosen a manner of introducing yourself which is hardly a recommendation,' she said, 'even were I in the habit of making acquaintances, which I am not. Pray allow me to continue my walk. Come, Flossie, pick up your basket, and come with mamma.'

'How can you be so cruel?' he asked, almost piteously. 'Why are you so determined to avoid me? I am not a scoundrel or a snob. If my mode of approaching you to-day seems ungentlemanlike—'

'Seems!' she repeated, with languid scorn.

'If it *is* ungentlemanlike, you must consider that there is no other means open to me. Have I not earned some kind of right to address you by the constancy of my worship, by the unalterable devotion which has made me follow you from town to town, patiently waiting for some happy hour like this, in which I should find myself face to face with you?'

'I do not know whether I ought to feel grateful for what you call your devotion,' she said coldly; 'but I can only say that I consider it very disagreeable to be followed from town to town in the manner you speak of, and that I shall be extremely obliged if you will discontinue your most useless pursuit.'

'Must it be always useless? Is there no hope for me? My letters have told you who and what I am, and what I have dared to hope.'

'Your letters?'

'Yes; you have received them, have you not?'

'I have received some very foolish letters. Are you the writer?'

'Yes; I am Geoffrey Hossack.'

'And you go about the world, Mr. Hossack, asking ladies of whom you know nothing whatever to marry you,' she replied, looking him full in the face, with a penetrating look in the full clear gray eyes—eyes which reminded him curiously of other eyes, yet he knew not whose.

'Upon my honour, madam,' he answered gravely, and with an earnest warmth that attested his sincerity, 'you are the first and the only woman I ever asked to be my wife.'

That truthful tone, those candid eyes boldly meeting her gaze, may have touched her. A faint crimson flushed her cheek, and her eyelids drooped. It was the first sign of emotion he had seen in her face.

'If that be true, I can only acknowledge the honour of your preference, and regret that you have wasted so much devotion upon one who can never be anything more than a stranger to you.'

Geoffrey shot a swift glance after the child before opening the floodgates of his passion. Blessed innocent, she had strayed off to a distant patch of sunlit verdure carpeted with wild hyacinths—'the heavens upbreaking through the earth.'

'Never?' he echoed; 'never more than a stranger? Is it wise to make so light of an honest passion—a love that is strong to suffer or to dare? Put me to the test, Mrs. Bertram. I don't ask you to trust me or believe in me all at once. God knows I will be patient. Only look me in the face and say, "Geoffrey Hossack, you may hope," and I will abide your will for all the rest. I will follow you with a spaniel's fidelity, worship you with the blind idolatry of an Indian fakir; will do for you what I should never dream of doing for myself—strive to win reputation and position. Fortune has been won for me.'

'Were you the Lord Chancellor,' she said, with a slow sad smile, 'it would make no difference. You and I can never be more than strangers, Mr. Hossack. I am sorry for your foolish infatuation, just as I should pity a spoiled child who cried for the moon. But that young moon sailing cold and dim in the sky yonder is as near to you as I can ever be.'

'I won't believe it!' he exclaimed passionately, feeling very much like that spoiled child who will not forego his desire for the moon. 'Give me only a chance. Do not be so cruel as to refuse me your friendship: let me see you sometimes, as you might if we had met in society. Forgive me for my audacity in approaching you as I have done to-day. Remember it was only by such a step I could cross the barrier that divides us. I have waited so long for this opportunity: for pity's sake do not tell me that I have waited in vain.'

He stood bareheaded in the fading sunlight—young, handsome—his candid face glowing with fervour and truth; a piteous appealing expression in those eyes that had been wont to look out upon life with so gay and hopeful a glance,—not a man to be lightly scorned, it would seem; not a wooer whose loyal passion a wise woman would have spurned.

'I can only repeat what I have already told you,' Mrs. Bertram said quietly, as unmoved by his appeal as if beneath her statuesque beauty there had been nothing but marble; no pitiful impulsive woman's heart to be melted by his warmth, or touched by his self-abasement. 'Nothing could be more foolish or more useless than this fancy—'

'Fancy!' he repeated bitterly. 'It is the one heartfelt passion of a lifetime, and you call it fancy!'

'Nothing could be more foolish,' she went on,

regardless of his interruption. 'I cannot accept your friendship in the present; I cannot contemplate the possibility of returning your affection in the future. My path in life lies clear and straight before me—very narrow, very barren, perhaps—and it must be trodden in solitude, except for that dear child. Forget your mistaken admiration for one who has done nothing to invite it. Go back to the beaten way of life. What is that Byron says, Byron who had drained the cup of all passions? Love makes so little in a man's existence. You are young, rich, unfettered, with all the world before you, Mr. Hossack. Thank God for so many blessings, and'—with a little laugh that had some touch of bitterness—'do not cry for the moon.'

She left him, with a grave inclination of the proud head, and went away to look for her child—left him planted there, ashamed of himself and his failure; loving her desperately, yet desperately angry with her; ready, had there only been a loaded pistol within reach, to blow his brains out on the spot.

CHAPTER VII.

'SORROW HAS NEED OF FRIENDS.'

GEOFFREY went to the concert at the Stillmington Assembly Rooms that evening, his disappointment notwithstanding. Granted that he had comported himself in a mean and cad-like fashion; granted that this woman he loved was colder than granite, unapproachable as the rocky spurs of Australian mountains, whose sheer height the foot of man has never scaled; granted that his passion was of all follies the maddest,—he loved her still. That one truth remained, unshaken and abiding, fixed as the centre of this revolving globe. He loved her.

The audience at the Assembly Rooms that evening was not large; indeed, Stillmington spent so much money upon gentility as to have little left for pleasure. The Stillmingtonites visited one another in closed flies, which were solemnly announced towards the end of each entertainment as Colonel or Mr. So-and-so's carriage. The distance that divided their several abodes was of the smallest, yet he was a daring innovator who ventured to take his wife on foot to a Stillmington dinner-party, rather than immure her during the brief journey in one of Spark's flies. Concerts, however, the Stillmingtonites approved as a fashionable and aristocratic form of entertainment—not boisterously amusing, and appealing to the higher orders, for the most part through the genteel medium of foreign languages. There was generally, therefore, a fair sprinkling of the *élite* of Stillmington in the Assembly Room on such occasions, and there was a fair sprinkling to-night—a faint flutter of fans, an assortment of patrician shoulders draped with opera cloaks of white or crimson; an imposing display of elderly gentlemen with shining bald heads and fierce gray whiskers; and, on the narrower benches devoted to the vulgar herd, a sparse assemblage of tradesmen's wives and daughters in their best bonnets.

Geoffrey Hossack sat amongst the *élite*, sick at heart, yet full of eager longing, of feverish expectancy, knowing that his only hope now was to see her thus, that the fond vain dream of being something nearer to her was ended. Nothing was left him but the privilege of dogging her footsteps, of gazing at her from among the crowd, of hearing the sweet voice whose Circean strains had wrought this madness in his mind, of following her to the end of life with his obnoxious love.

'I shall become a modern Wandering Jew,' he thought, 'and she will hate me. I shall provoke her with my odious presence till she passes from indifference to aversion. I can't help it. My destiny is to love her, and a man can but fulfil his destiny.'

She sang the old Italian song he loved so well—that melody whose pathetic tones have breathed their sad sweetness into so many ears—recalling fond memories and vain regrets, thoughts of a love that has been and is no more, or lives only beyond the grave.

To Geoffrey those pensive strains spoke of love in the present—love dominant, triumphant in its springtide of force and passion.

'Voi che sapéte che cosa è amor,' he repeated to himself bitterly; 'I should rather think I did. It's the only thing I do know in the present obfuscation of my faculties.'

Their eyes met once in the look she cast round the room. Great Heaven, what regretful tenderness in hers! Such a look as that maddened him. Had she but looked at him thus to-day in the garden, he would surely have done something desperate—clasped her in his arms, and sworn to carry her to the uttermost ends of the earth, if thereby he might be sure of his prize. Could she look at him thus, she who had been colder than the icy breath of the polar seas, when he had pleaded with all the force of his passion two short hours ago?

His eyes never left her face while she sang. When she vanished, the platform was a blank. Other performers came and went; there was other music, vocal and instrumental—to him it seemed no more than the vague murmur of a far-off waterfall in the ears of slumber. She came back again, after an interval that seemed intolerably long, and sang something of Balfe's—a poem by Longfellow, called 'Daybreak'— mournful, like most of her songs, but full of music.

During the interval between the two concerts Geoffrey paced Stillmington and its environs with an indefatigable industry that might have shamed the local postman, for *he* at least was weary, while Geoffrey knew not weariness. Vainly did he haunt that aristocratic High-street, vainly linger by the door of the circulating library, the fancy repository, the music-shop where somebody was perpetually trying pianos with woolly basses and tinkling trebles; vainly did he stroll in and out of the garden where he had dared to molest Mrs. Bertram with his unwelcome adoration,—she was nowhere to be met with.

One comfort only remained to him, a foolish one, like all those fancies whence love derives consolation. He knew where his enchantress lived, and in the quiet dusk, when the gentle hush of evening enfolded Stillmington like a mantle, he would venture to pace the lonely street beneath her windows; would watch her taper gleaming faintly in that gray nightfall which was not yet darkness, would, as it were, project his spirit into her presence, and keep her company in spite of herself.

The street where she lodged was on the outskirts of the town, newly built—a street of commonplace dwellings of the speculative builder's pattern; a row of square boxes, with not a variation of an inch from number one to number thirty; sordid, unpicturesque: habitations which even love could not beautify. Mrs. Bertram occupied the upper floor above a small haberdasher's shop, such a shop as one felt could be kept only by a widow—a scanty display of poor feminine trifles in the window, children's pinafores, cheap gloves, cheap artificial flowers, cheap finery of divers kinds, whose unsubstantial fabric a spring shower would reduce to mere pulp or rag useless even for the paper-mill.

Here, between seven and eight o'clock, Mr. Hossack used to smoke his after-dinner cigar, despairing yet deriving a dismal pleasure from the sense of his vicinity to the beloved, like those who, in the gloaming, pace a churchyard within whose pale their treasure lies. The twinkling light shining palely athwart the white blind cheered him a little. Her hand had perhaps kindled it. She was there alone—for Geoffrey, in whom the parental instinct was unawakened, did not count a child as company—amidst those humble surroundings, she whose loveliness would enhance the splendour of a palace. Thus, with all love's exaggeration, he thought of her.

One evening he was bold enough to penetrate the little shop. 'Had they any gloves that would fit him?—eights or nines he believed he required.' As he had supposed, the shopkeeper was a widow. She emerged from the little parlour at the back, dressed in rusty weeds, to assist a young woman with a small pinched visage and corkscrew ringlets, who was feebly groping among the shelves and little paper packets with hieroglyphical labels.

'Lor, Matilda Jane, you never know where to find anything! There's a parcel of drab men's on that top shelf. I'm sorry to keep you waiting, sir. We have a large selection of cloth and lisle-thread gloves. You'd like lisle-thread, perhaps, as the weather's setting in so warm?'

'Yes, lisle-thread will do,' answered Geoffrey, who had never worn anything but Jouvin's best, at five shillings a pair.

He seated himself, and looked round the stuffy little shop. Above this gloomy den Mrs. Bertram lived. He listened for her light step while the drab men's were being hunted for.

'I think you have one of the ladies who sang at the concert lodging with you?' said this hypocrite, while he made believe to try on the thread gloves.

'Yes, sir; Mrs. Bertram: a very sweet young person; so mild and affable.'

'But not chatty, mother,' interjected the damsel in ringlets. 'It's as much as one can do to get half-a-dozen words out of her; and it's my belief she's as proud as she can be, in spite of her soft voice.'

'Hold your tongue, Matilda Jane; you're always running people down,' remonstrated the matron. 'I think that pair will fit you nicely, sir,' as Geoffrey thrust his strong fingers into the limp thread. 'Poor dear lady, there wasn't much pride left in her this morning, when she spoke to me about her little girl.'

'Her little girl! There is nothing the matter, I hope?'

'Yes, sir, there is. The poor little dear has took

the scarlatina. Where she could have took it, I can't imagine; for it's not in this street: indeed, we're very free from everything except measles in this part of the town; and they're everywhere, as you may say, where there's children. But the little girl has took the scarlatina somehow, and Mrs. Bertram's dreadful down-hearted about it. The poor child's got it rather bad, I grant you; but then, as I tell her mar, it's only scarlatina: those things ending with a "tina" are never dangerous—it isn't as if it was scarlet-fever.'

'You are sure the child is in no danger?' cried Geoffrey anxiously; not that he cared for children in the abstract; but *her* child—a priceless treasure, doubtless—*that* must not be imperilled.

'No, sir; indeed I don't think as there's any danger. I'll allow the fever's been very high, and the child has been brought down by it; but the doctor hasn't hinted at danger. He is to look in again this evening.'

'He comes twice a day, does he? That looks as if the case were serious.'

'It was Mrs. Bertram's wish, sir. Feeling anxious like, she asked him.'

Geoffrey was silent for a few minutes, meditating. If he could establish some kind of *rapport* between himself and these people, it would be something gained: he would feel himself nearer to his beloved in her affliction. Alas, that she should be sorrowful, and he powerless to comfort her; so much a stranger to her, that any expression of sympathy would seem an impertinence!

'I have heard Mrs. Bertram sing a great many times,' he said, 'and have been charmed with her singing. I am deeply interested in her (as a musical amateur), and in anything that concerns her welfare. I shall venture to call again to-morrow evening, to inquire how the little girl is going on. But pray do not mention me to Mrs. Bertram; I am quite unknown to her, and the idea that a stranger had expressed an interest in her might be displeasing. I'll take half-a-dozen pairs of gloves.'

He threw down a sovereign—a delightful coin, which not often rang upon that humble counter. The widow emptied her till in order to find change for this lavish customer.

'Half-a-dozen gloves, at fifteenpence, seven-and-sixpence. Thank you, sir. Is there anything in socks or pocket-handkerchiefs I can show you?'

'Not to-night, thanks. I'll look at some handkerchiefs to-morrow,' said Geoffrey; and departed, rejoiced to find that by the expenditure of a few shillings he could keep himself informed of Mrs. Bertram's movements.

He went straight to the best fruiterer in the town, whose shop was on the point of closing. Here he bought some hot-house grapes, at fourteen shillings a pound, which he dispatched at once to Mrs. Bertram's lodging. He had sent her his tribute of choice flowers continually, in the course of his long pursuit, but she had never deigned to wear a blossom of his sending.

She was to sing on the following evening. 'If her child is worse, she will not appear,' he thought. But when he called at the little shop that afternoon, he heard the child was somewhat better, and that she meant to sing.

'There was some grapes came last night, sir, soon after you left,' said the widow. 'Was it you that sent them? Mrs. Bertram seemed so pleased. The poor little thing was parched with fever, and the grapes was such a comfort.'

'You didn't say anything about me?' said Geoffrey.

'Not a syllable, sir.'

'That's right. I'll send more grapes. If there is anything else I can do, pray let me know. I'm such a stupid fellow. You may send me a dozen of those handkerchiefs,'—without looking at the fabric, which was about good enough for his groom. 'I shall be so grateful to you if you can suggest anything that I could do for the little girl.'

'I don't think there's anything, sir. Her mar lets her want for nothing. But the grapes was a surprise. "I didn't think there were any to be had," Mrs. Bertram said. But perhaps she'd hardly go to the price, sir; for she doesn't seem to be very well off.'

Pinched by poverty! What a pang the thought gave him! And he squandered his useless means without being able to purchase contentment. He had been happy enough, certainly, in his commonplace way, before he had seen her; but now that he had tasted the misery of loving her, he could not go back to that empty happiness—the joy of vulgar minds, which need only vulgar pleasures.

He was in his seat in the front row when the concert began. Whatever musical faculty might be latent in his composition stood a fair chance of development nowadays, so patiently did he sit out pianoforte solos, concertante duets, trios for piano, violin, and 'cello; warblings, soprano and contralto, classical or modern; hearing all alike with the same callous ear till she appeared—a tall slim figure simply robed;

a sad sweet face, full of a quiet pride that seemed to hold him aloof, yet with that fleeting look of love and pity in those tender eyes which seemed to draw him near.

To-night that serious countenance was in his eyes supremely pathetic; for he knew her secret sorrow, knew that her heart was with her sick child.

She sang one of the old familiar songs—nothing classical, only an old-fashioned English ballad, 'She wore a wreath of roses,' a simple sentimental story of love and sorrow. The plaintive notes moved many to tears, even the Stillmingtonites, who were not easily melted, being too eminently genteel for emotion.

'Good heavens, what a fool she makes of me!' thought Geoffrey; 'I who never cared a straw for music.'

He waited near a little door at the back of the Assembly Rooms, by which he knew the concert people went in and out—waited until Mrs. Bertram emerged, one of the earliest. She was not alone. Her landlady's daughter, the young woman in corkscrew ringlets, accompanied her. He followed them at a respectful distance, observed by neither.

Pity and impetuous love made him bold. No sooner were they in a quiet unfrequented street than he quickened his pace, came up with them, and dared once more to address the woman who had scorned him.

'Forgive me, Mrs. Bertram,' he said. 'I have heard of your little girl's illness, and I am so anxious to know if I can be of any use to you. Is there anything I can do?'

'Nothing,' she answered sadly, not slackening her pace for a moment. 'It is kind of you to wish to help me, but unless you could give my darling health and strength—she was so well and strong only a few days ago—you can do nothing. She is in God's hands; I must be patient. I daresay it is only a childish illness, which need not make me miserable. But—but she is all the world to me.'

'Are you satisfied with your doctor, or shall I get you other medical advice? I will telegraph to London for any one you would like to have.'

'You are very kind,' she answered gently, her manner strangely different from what it had been in the garden. 'No; I have no reason to be dissatisfied with the doctor who is attending my pet. He is kind, and seems clever. I thank you for your wish to help me in my trouble. Good-night.'

They were in the street where she lived by this time. She made him a little curtsy, and passed on very quickly to the shop door, and vanished from his eager eyes. He paced the street for an hour, watching the light in the two little windows above the shop, before he went back to his hotel, and for him the night was sleepless. How could he rest while she was unhappy?

CHAPTER VIII.

GEOFFREY INCLINES TO SUSPICION.

Towards morning self-indulgent habits triumphed over anxious love. After tossing all night in feverish unrest, Mr. Hossack slept soundly till noon; but not a commonplace slumber, for the visions of his head upon his bed were made beautiful to him by the image of his beloved. She was with him in that dreamworld where all is smooth and fair as the wide bosom of Danube when no storm-wind ruffles his waters; a world where there were neither sick children nor concerts—nothing but happiness and love.

He awakened himself reluctantly from so sweet a delusion, dressed and breakfasted hurriedly, and went straight to the little draper's shop at the fag end of Stillmington. After Mrs. Bertram's gentler manner last night, he felt as if he might venture to approach her. Sorrow had brought them nearer to each other; she who had so sternly repulsed his love had not rejected his sympathy. She had thanked him, even, for his proffered aid, in that thrilling voice which in speech as in song went straight to his heart.

The young woman was behind the counter when he went in, reading a number of the *London Journal* in pensive solitude.

'How is the little girl this morning?' he asked eagerly.

'O, sir, I'm sorry to say she's not so well. She was light-headed last night, and her poor mar sat up, and looks as pale as a ghost to-day, and the doctor seemed more serious like. But as mother tells Mrs. Bertram, it's only scarlatina; it isn't as if it was scarlet fever, you know.'

The little door of communication between the shop and the staircase opened at this moment, and Jane Bertram's pale face appeared—how pale and wan! He could not have thought one night's suffering would have worked such a change.

'She is worse,' she said, looking at the girl with haggard eyes that hardly seemed to have sight in them. 'For God's sake run for the doctor.'

'She can't be so bad as all that. Come, bear up, Mrs. Bertram, that's a dear,' answered the girl kindly. 'You're so nervous, and you're not used to illness. I'll run and fetch Mr. Vincent if you like, but I daresay there's no need.'

She shuffled on her bonnet as she spoke.

'I don't know,' Mrs. Bertram said helplessly; 'I don't know what I ought to do; she was never so ill before.'

She went up-stairs, Geoffrey following, emboldened by pity. He stood by the open door of the little bedroom—commonly furnished, but neat and spotless in its pure drapery of white dimity, its well-scrubbed floor, and freshly-papered wall. The sick child lay with her golden hair spread loosely on the pillow, her blue eyes bright with fever. The landlady sat by the bed, sharing the mother's watch.

Mrs. Bertram bent over the child, kissed her with fond passionate kisses, and murmured broken words of love, then turned towards the door, surprised to see the intruder.

'You here!' she exclaimed, seeing Geoffrey, but with no anger in the sorrowful face.

'Yes, I want so much to be of use to you. Will you spare me two minutes, in here?' he asked, pointing to the sitting-room, the door of which stood open. 'The little girl is safe with our good friend.'

'Yes,' the mother answered piteously. 'I can do nothing for her. Only God can help us—only He who pitied the sinful woman in her agony.'

The words struck strangely on his ear, but he

let them pass unnoticed as the wild cry of an almost despairing soul. What should she have to do with sin? she in whose countenance reigned purity and a proud innocence none could dare impeach.

'I spoke to you last night about getting farther advice,' he said. 'Mind, I don't suppose it's in the least degree necessary; your child's recovery is no doubt merely a question of time. These childish fevers must run their course. But I can see that you are unduly anxious. It might be a comfort to you to see another doctor, a man especially experienced in the treatment of children. I know just such a man—one who has been particularly successful with children; not an eminent man by any means, but one who has worked among the poor, whose heart is in his profession, whose work is really a labour of love. I can speak of him with perfect confidence, for he is my friend, and I know all this to be true. Let me telegraph for him; I am sure that he will come as quickly as an express train can bring him.'

Her eyes brightened a little, and she gave him a look full of gratitude.

'How good of you to think of this!' she said. 'O yes, pray, pray send for him. Such a man as that might save my darling, even if she were in danger, and the doctor here says there is no danger. Pray send for this good man. I am not very rich, but I will gladly pay any fee within my means, and be his debtor for farther payment in the future.'

'He will not want payment,' answered Geoffrey, with a smile. 'He is my friend, and would make a longer journey than from London here to serve me. Rely upon it, he will be with you before this evening. Good-bye, Mrs. Bertram, and try to be hopeful. If I thought there were a better man in all London than the man I am going to summon, rely upon it I would have that better man.'

He gave her his hand, which she did not refuse; at least, she let her feverish little hand rest in his for one brief delicious moment, perhaps unconsciously. But he felt that he had gained ground since that day in the garden. He had won the right to approach her.

He jumped into the first fly he met, told the man to drive his hardest to the railway station—it was before the days of postal telegraph offices—and dispatched his message, paying for both telegram and reply.

The message ran thus:

'*From Geoffrey Hossack, Stillmington, Warwickshire, to Lucius Davoren, 103 Shadrack-road, London.*

'Come here at once to see a sick child. No time

to be lost. Your coming quickly will be the greatest favour you can do me. The patient's address is 15 Marlow-street, New-town, Stillmington. Answer paid for.'

The telegram handed over to the clerk, he began to speculate upon the probabilities of delay. After all, this telegraphic system, which would have seemed so miraculous to our ancestors, is not rapid enough for the impatience of Young England's impetuous spirit.

It seems a slow business at the best. Science has made the matter swift as light, but clerkly sluggishness and slow-footed messengers clog electricity's wings, and a message which takes a hundred seconds for its actual transmission from the operator to the dial may not be delivered for a couple of hours.

Geoffrey went back to Marlow-street to hear the last tidings of the little patient. She was sleeping peacefully, and her mother seemed more hopeful. This lightened his heart a good deal, and he went back to his hotel, smoked a cigar, played a game at pyramids with some officers from the Stillmington Barracks, and thus beguiled the time until a waiter brought him the answer to his telegram. It was brief and decisive:

'I shall come to Stillmington by the last train. Must see patients before leaving.'

The last train! That meant considerable delay. It was now four o'clock, and the last train came into Stillmington at eleven. How coolly these doctors take things! Geoffrey felt as if his friend ought to have abandoned all his other patients to their fates for the sake of this sick child. The last train! Was this the measure of friendship?

Happily the latest report of the little girl was cheering. Doubtless all would be well. On the strength of this hope Geoffrey dined; and dined tolerably well, having asked the officers to share his meal. This hospitality prolonged the business of dining till after nine o'clock, when Geoffrey pleaded an engagement as an excuse for getting rid of his guests, and went for the third time that day to Marlow-street. He had drunk little or nothing at the social board, and had felt the exercise of hospitality somewhat irksome; but he was the kind of young man to whom dinner-giving is an absolute necessity.

The draper's shop in Marlow-street had closed its shutters, but the door stood open, and the damsel in ringlets was airing herself on the threshold after the labours of a day which had brought her about half a dozen customers.

To Geoffrey's question, which had become almost a formula, she answered hopefully. The child was better. She had sat up for a minute and had drunk a cup of milk, and had taken sundry spoonfuls of beef-tea, and had eaten three grapes, and had spoken 'quite lively and sensible-like. Children are so soon down, and so soon up again,' said the damsel. 'It's no good taking on about them, as I told Mrs. Bertram this morning.'

'She is happier now, I suppose,' said Geoffrey.

'O dear, yes, quite herself again.'

'Will you ask her if I may see her for a minute or two? I want to tell her about the doctor I have sent for.'

The girl went up-stairs and returned speedily.

'Mrs. Bertram will be happy to see you,' she said, 'if you'll please to walk up.'

If he would please to walk up! Would he please to enter paradise, did its gates stand open for him? To see her even in her grief was sweet as a foretaste of heaven. She received him this evening with a smile.

'God has heard my prayer,' she said; 'my little darling is better. I really don't think I need have troubled your kind friend to come down. I begin to feel more confidence in Mr. Vincent, now that my treasure is better.'

'I am rejoiced to hear it. But my friend will be here to-night. He is one of the best of men. He saved my life once under circumstances of much hardship and danger. We have faced death together. I should not be here to tell you this but for Lucius Davoren.'

'Lucius Davoren!' She repeated the name with a wondering look, horror-stricken, her hand clutching the back of the chair from which she had risen. 'Is your friend's name Lucius Davoren?'

'Yes. Can it be possible that you know him? That would be very strange.'

'No,' she said slowly; 'I do not know this friend of yours. But his name is associated with a somewhat painful memory.'

'Very painful, I fear, or you would hardly have grown so pale at the mention of his name,' said Geoffrey, with a jealous horror of anything like a secret in his divinity's past life.

'I was foolish to be agitated by such a trifle. After all it's only a coincidence. I daresay there are a good many Davorens in the world,' she answered carelessly.

'I doubt it. Davoren is not a common name.'

'Has your friend, this Mr. Lucius Davoren, been successful in life?'

'I can hardly say that. As I told you when I first spoke of him, he is by no means distinguished. He is indeed almost at the beginning of his professional career. Yet were I racked with the most obscure of diseases, I should laugh all your specialists to scorn and cry, "Send for Lucius Davoren."'

'He is poor, I suppose?' she asked curiously.

'Very likely; in the sense of having no money for luxury, splendour, or pleasure—things which he holds in sovereign contempt. He can afford to give the best years of his youth to patient labour among the poor. That is the education he has chosen for himself, rather than a West-end practice and a single brougham; and I believe he will find it the shortest road to everlasting fame.'

'I am glad you believe in him,' she said warmly, 'since he is such a great man.'

'But you have not yet recovered from the shock his name caused you just now.'

'Not quite. My darling's illness has made me nervous. If you think your friend will not be offended, I would rather avoid seeing him,' she added, in a pleading tone. 'I really don't feel well enough to see a stranger. I have passed through such alternations of hope and fear during the ast few days. Will your friend forgive me if I leave Mrs. Grabbit to receive his instructions? She is a good soul, and will forget nothing he tells her.'

'Do just as you like,' replied Geoffrey, mystified, and somewhat disturbed in mind by this proposition; 'of course you needn't see him unless you please. But he's a very good fellow, and my truest friend. I should like you to have made his acquaintance. You'll think me a selfish beg—fellow for saying so; but I really believe you'd have a better opinion of me if you knew Lucius Davoren. His friendship is a kind of certificate. But of course, if you'd rather not see him, there's an end of it. I'll tell him that you have unpleasant associations with his name, and that the very mention of it agitated you.'

'No!' she cried, with a vehemence that startled him. 'For God's sake say nothing, tell him nothing, except that I am too ill to see any one. I detest anything like fuss. And why make a mountain out of the veriest molehill? His name reminded me of past sorrow, that is all.'

'Capricious,' thought Geoffrey; 'with a temper by no means as regular as the classic beauty of her face, I daresay. But were she as violent as Shakespeare's shrew before Petruchio tamed her, I should not the less adore her. Past sorrow! Some doctor called Davoren may have attended her husband on his death-bed. She is just the kind of woman to lock her heart up in a tomb, and then go about the world luring mankind to their destruction by her calm passionless beauty, and answering all with the same dismal sentence, "My heart is with the dead."'

He submitted to Mrs. Bertram's decision. He promised to meet his friend at the station, bring him straight to the sick-room, and with his own hand carry Mr. Davoren's prescription to the chief chemist of Stillmington.

And thus he left her; perplexed, but not all unhappy. Blessings on that sweet child for her timeous indisposition! It had opened the way to his acquaintance with the mother; an acquaintance which, beginning with service and sympathy, promised to ripen quickly into friendship.

The last train brought Lucius. The friends met with a strong hand-grasp, a few hearty words of greeting, and then walked swiftly from the station, which, after the manner of provincial stations, had been placed a good half mile from the town, for the advantage of local fly-drivers, no doubt, and the livery-stable interest.

'And pray who is this small patient in whose welfare you are so concerned, Geoff?' asked Lucius.

'Has some piteous case of local distress awakened your dormant philanthropy? I know you're a good fellow, but I didn't know you went in for district-visiting.'

'There's no philanthropy in the question, Lucius. Only selfish, pig-headed love. I say pig-headed, because the lady doesn't value my affection; scorns it, in fact. But I hold on with a bulldog pertinacity. After all, you see, an Englishman's highest quality is his bulldoggedness.'

'But what has your bulldog affection to do with a sick child?'

'Heaven bless the little innocent! One would suppose she had fallen ill on purpose to bring about my acquaintance with her most unapproachable mother. Don't you remember my telling you that Mrs. Bertram has a little girl—a red-legged angel, after Millais?'

'O, yes, by the way, there was a child,' said Lucius indifferently. Then warming as he contemplated the case in its professional aspect, 'She is not very ill, I hope?'

'Scarlatina,' replied Geoffrey. 'But she seems to be mending to-night.'

'Scarlatina!' exclaimed Lucius; 'and you brought me down to Stillmington to see a case of scarlatina, which any local apothecary would understand just as well as I!'

'You dear old fellow! don't be angry. It wasn't so much the scarlatina. I wanted you to see Mrs. Bertram. I wanted you to see with your own eyes that the woman I love is worthy of any man's affection.'

'And you think I should be in a position to decide that question after half-an-hour's acquaintance? A question which has taken some men a lifetime to solve, and which some have left unanswered at their death. No, Geoff, I don't pretend to be wiser than other men where a woman's character is in question. And if my instinct warned me against your enchantress, and if I should advise you speedily to forget her, how much do you think my counsel would influence you?'

'Not much, I'm afraid, Lucius. It wouldn't be very easy for me to cast off her thrall. I am her willing bondslave. Nothing less than the knowledge that she is unworthy of my love—that her past life holds some dishonourable secret—would change my purpose. She has left my letters unanswered, she has rejected my offered devotion, and with something like scorn; yet there has been a look in her face, more transient than an April sunbeam, that has given me hope. I mean to hold on—I mean to win her love—in spite of herself, if need be.'

He gave a brief sketch of that little scene in the garden, his audacity, her almost contemptuous indifference; and then explained how Fortune, or, as he put it, the scarlatina, had smiled upon him.

'And you think, notwithstanding her affected indifference, that she loves you?'

'Loves is too strong a word. What have I done to merit her love, except follow her as a collie follows a flock of sheep? What is there in me to deserve or attract her love? I am not ravishingly beautiful. I do not sing with a heart-penetrating voice. It is only natural I should worship her. It is the old story of the moon and the water brooks.'

'But you talked about a look which gave you hope.'

'A look! Yes, Davoren. Such a look—sorrow and tenderness, regret, despair, all blended in one swift glance from those divine eyes—a look that might madden a man. Such a look as Paris may have seen in Helen's eyes before he planned the treason that ended in flaming Troy. But after all it may have meant nothing; it may have existed only in my wild imagining. When a man is as deep in love as I am, Heaven only knows to what hallucinations he may be subject.'

'Well,' said Lucius cheerily, with that practical spirit which men bring to bear upon other men's passions, 'I shall see the lady, and be able at least to form some opinion as to whether she loves you or not. Whether she be worthy of your love is a question I would not attempt to solve, but the other is easier. I think I shall discover if she loves you. What a pleasant smell of the country—newly-turned earth and budding hedgerows—there is about here! It refreshes my senses after the odours of the Shadrack-road, where we have a wonderful combination of bone-burning, tan-yard, and soap-caldron.'

'I am glad you enjoy the country air,' said Geoffrey, in a somewhat sheepish tone, 'and I do hope you'll be able to spare to-morrow for a dog-cart exploration of the neighbourhood, as that may atone for my having brought you here somewhat on a fool's errand. The fact is, Mrs. Bertram would rather not see you.'

'Rather not see the doctor who has come from London to attend her sick child! An odd kind of mother.'

'You're wrong, Lucius; she's a most devoted mother. I never saw any one so broken down as she was this morning, before the little thing took a turn for the better. Don't run away with any false notion of that kind; she idolises that child. Only she has knocked herself up with nursing; and she has been alarmed, and agitated, and, in short, isn't in a fit state to see any one.'

'Except you,' said Lucius.

'My dear fellow, in her distress about the child she has thought no more of me than if I were—a—a gingham umbrella,' said Geoffrey, after casting about wildly for a comparison. 'She thinks of nothing but that red-legged angel. And you can imagine that at such a moment she would shrink from seeing a stranger.'

'Even the doctor who comes to see her child. She is the first mother I ever knew to act in such a manner. Don't be angry with me, Geoff, if I say that this looks to me very much as if your divinity feared to trust herself to eyes less blind than yours —as if she knew there is that in herself, or in her life, which would not impress a dispassionate observer favourably. Your blind worship has made her a goddess. She doesn't want to come down from her pedestal in the shadowy temple of your imagination into the broad glare of every-day life.'

Of course Geoffrey was angry. Was he a fool, or

a schoolboy, to be caught by meretricious charms—to take tinsel for gold?

'I have seen women enough in my time to know a good one when I meet one; and that this woman is good and true I will stake my life, my hope of winning her even, which is dearer to me than life.'

'And if you found her less than you believe her, you would do what you said three months ago—pluck her out of your heart?'

'Yes, though her jesses were my heartstrings.'

'Good; that's all I want to know. I tell you frankly, Geoff, I don't like this wandering apprenticeship to your new divinity. I don't like the idea of a life-passion picked up by the roadside—of all your hopes of future happiness being grounded upon a woman of whom you know absolutely nothing.'

'Only that she is the noblest woman I ever met,' said Geoffrey doggedly.

'Which means that she has a handsome face,' said the other.

CHAPTER IX.

SOMETHING TOO MUCH FOR GRATITUDE.

By this time Mr. Hossack and his friend had come from the pleasant country road into the shabbiest outskirt of Stillmington, that outskirt which contained Marlow-street. Strange that even in so select a town as Stillmington, Poverty will set up its tents.

The shop had been shut some time, but the door stood ajar, and a light burnt dimly within. Geoffrey and his companion were expected. Miss Grabbit was yawning over a tattered novel in her accustomed place behind the counter.

'O, is it the doctor, sir?' she exclaimed, brightening. 'Will you walk up-stairs, please? Mother's with the little girl, and she's been sleeping beautiful. I feel sure she's took a turn.'

'Is Mrs. Bertram up-stairs?' asked Geoffrey.

'No, she's lying down a bit on our sofa in there,' pointing to the closed door of communication between the shop and parlour. 'She was right down worn out, and mother persuaded her to try and get a little rest. Mother will take all your directions, sir,' she added to Lucius.

That gentleman bowed, but said nothing. A curious mother this! The mothers he knew were wont to hang upon his words as on the sacred sentences of an oracle. He followed Geoffrey up the narrow stairs to the little bedroom where the child lay asleep. The pure spotless look of the small chamber struck him, and the beauty of the child's face was no common beauty. There was something in it which impressed him curiously — something that seemed familiar—familiar as a half-remembered dream. Good Heaven, was it not his dead sister's face that this one recalled to him—the face of the little sister who died years ago?

The fancy moved him deeply; and his hand trembled a little as he lightly raised the bedclothes from the child's throat and chest, with that gentle touch of the doctor's skilful hand, and bent down to listen to the breathing. All was satisfactory. He went through his examination calmly enough, that transient emotion once conquered; felt the slender wrist, performed that unpleasant operation with a silver spoon to which we have all submitted our unwilling throats at divers periods, and then pronounced that all was going on well.

He had gone round the bed to the side facing the door, in order to get nearer to his patient, who lay nearer this side than the other. He sat by the pillow, and gave his directions to Mrs. Grabbit without looking up from the little girl, whose hot hand lay gently held in his, while his grave eyes were bent upon the small fever-flushed face. Geoffrey had entered softly during the last few moments, and stood at the foot of the bed.

When Lucius had finished his instructions as to treatment, he looked up.

The door opposite the bed was open, and a woman stood upon the threshold—a tall slim figure dressed in black, a pale anxious face, beautiful even in its sadness.

At sight of that silent figure, the surgeon started from his seat with a smothered cry of surprise. The sad eyes met his steadily with an imploring look, a look that for him spoke plainly enough.

Geoffrey looked at him wonderingly, perplexed by that startled movement.

'What's the matter?' he asked.

'Nothing. But I saw a lady looking in at that door. The mother perhaps.'

Geoffrey darted into the sitting-room. Yes she was there, standing by the window in the wan light of a week-old moon, with tears streaming down her face.

'My dear Mrs. Bertram, pray, pray do not distress yourself!' cried Geoffrey, to whom the office of consoler was new and strange. 'All is going on well; nothing could be more satisfactory—Lucius says so. She will be herself again in a few days.'

'Thank God, and thank your friend for me,' she said, in a voice choked with sobs. 'I could not rest downstairs; I wanted to hear what he said. Tell him I thank him with all my heart.'

'Thank him with your own lips,' pleaded Geoffrey; 'he will value your words far above mine. And you don't know what a good fellow he is.'

'Let Mrs. Bertram feel assured that I am only too happy to have been of use,' said the voice of Lucius from the threshold.

Mrs. Bertram hurried to the door, where the surgeon's figure stood, tall and dark, on the unlighted landing.

'O, let me speak to him, let me take his hand!' she cried, with uncontrollable agitation; and the next moment stood face to face with Lucius Davoren, with her hand clasped in his.

They could hardly see each other's faces, but

that was a lingering handclasp. Geoffrey stood a little way apart, watching them with some slight wonder, and thinking that quite so much gratitude could hardly be necessary even for a doctor who had travelled over a hundred miles to write a prescription for an idolised child.

'It's a pity I'm not in the medical line myself,' he thought, somewhat bitterly; and yet he had been anxious that Mrs. Bertram should acknowledge his friend's services.

He reflected that a doating mother was doubtless a foolish creature. He must not be angry with his divinity if she seemed hysterical, or even in a state bordering on distraction.

'Come, Lucius,' he said; 'Mrs. Bertram has gone through no end of agitation to-day, or rather yesterday, for it's past midnight. We had better leave her to rest.'

'Yes,' said Lucius, in a slow thoughtful tone, 'good-night. I will come to see the little girl again early to-morrow morning—say at eight o'clock—as I must leave Stillmington soon after nine.'

'O, come,' remonstrated Geoffrey, 'you must give yourself a holiday to-morrow.'

'Impossible. Pain and disease will not give my patients a holiday.'

'But surely their complaints can stand over for a day or so,' said Geoffrey. 'Parish patients can't have such complicated diseases. I thought all the worst evils flesh is heir to came from high living.'

'There are numerous diseases that come from low feeding, or almost no feeding at all. No; I must go back by an early train to-morrow. But I should like to see you at eight o'clock, if that will not be too soon, Mrs. Bertram.'

'Not at all too soon,' she answered; and they departed, Geoffrey with an uncomfortable foreboding that, so soon as the little girl recovered, his occupation would be gone. What other excuse could he find for intruding himself upon Mrs. Bertram's solitude?

'Well, Lucius,' he began, as soon as they were clear of the house, ' what do you think of her?'

'I think she is very handsome,' answered Lucius, with a thoughtful slowness which was peculiarly irritating to his friend. 'What more can I think of her after so brief an interview? She seems,' with an almost painful effort, ' very fond of her child. I am very sorry for her unprotected and solitary position; but—'

'But what?' cried Geoffrey impatiently. 'How you torment the soul of a fellow with your measured syllables!'

'I think the very wisest—nay, the only rational—thing you can do is to forget her.'

'Never! And why should I wish to forget her?'

'Because all surrounding circumstances point to the conclusion that she is no fitting wife for you. A woman so lovely, so accomplished, would hardly lead so lonely a life—I don't speak of her professional career, since that is a natural use for a woman to make of a fine voice if she wants to get her own living—if there were not some strong reason for her seclusion—some painful secret in the past, some fatal tie in the present. She knows you to be young, generous, wealthy, and her devoted slave; yet she rejects your devotion. She would scarcely repulse such a lover were she free to marry. Believe me, there is something in the background, some obstacle which you will never overcome. Be warned in time, my dear true-hearted Geoffrey; don't waste the best years of your life in the pursuit of a woman who can never reward your affection, who was not born to make you happy. There are plenty of women in the world quite as lovely, and—I won't say better worthy of you,' with ever so faint a quiver of his voice, 'but better able to bless your love.'

'When I meet such a woman I will forget her,'

answered the other. 'I thought you were a better judge of human nature, Lucius; I thought you would be able to recognise a good and pure woman when you saw one. True that you had seen very little of this one; yet you saw her with her fond mother's heart bared before you; you saw her warm and grateful nature. You had sneered at her as a heartless mother: see how facts belied your unkind suspicion. You saw her moved to passionate tears by the mere thought of your kindness to her child.'

'For God's sake, say no more about her!' cried Lucius, with sudden passion. 'The subject will breed a quarrel between us. You wanted my advice, and I have given it you—dispassionately. Reason, not feeling, has influenced my words. Pure, good, true: yes, I would willingly believe her all that, did I not—did not circumstances point to the other conclusion. It is hard to look in her face and say, This is not a woman to be loved and trusted. But are you the man to endure a shameful secret in your wife's past history? Could you face the hazard of some cruel discovery after marriage—a discovery which should show you the woman you love as a victim, perhaps, but not without guilt?'

'I will never believe her less than she seems to me at this moment!' cried Geoffrey. 'What makes you speculate on her past life? why suppose that there must be some ignominious secret? Only because she gets her own living, I suppose; because she is obliged to travel about the world without her own maid, and has no footman, or carriage, or circle of polite acquaintances, and possibly has never been presented at court. I wonder at you, Davoren; I could not have believed you were so narrow-minded.'

'Think me narrow-minded, if you like, but be warned by me. My voice to-night is the voice of the majority, which always takes the narrowest view of every question. You have asked for my advice, and you shall have it, however distasteful. Don't marry a woman of whom you know so little as you know about Mrs. Bertram.'

'Thanks for your advice. Of course I know you mean well, old fellow; but if Mrs. Bertram would take me for her husband to-morrow, I should be the proudest man in Stillmington, or in Christendom.'

'I think I know enough of her to feel very sure she will never consent to marry you,' said Lucius.

'You are quick in forming conclusions,' exclaimed Geoffrey, with a somewhat distrustful glance at his friend, 'considering that you saw Mrs. Bertram for something less than five minutes.'

They arrived at the hotel, where Geoffrey, although displeased with his friend, was not forgetful of hospitality's sacred rites. He ordered a spatchcock and a bottle of Roederer, and over this repast the two young men sat till late, talking of that subject which filled Geoffrey's heart and mind. Like a child, he was one moment angry with his friend, and in the next eager to hear all that Lucius could say about his passion and its object—eager for advice which he had no idea of following; bent upon proving, by love's eloquent oratory, that his divinity was all that is perfect among women. And so the night waned; and Geoffrey and his guest were the last among the inmates of that respectable family hotel to retire to their chambers in the long corridor, where the old-fashioned eight-day clock ticked solemnly in the deep of night.

Geoffrey would fain have presented himself in Marlow-street next morning with his friend, but having no reasonable excuse for visiting Mrs. Bertram at such an early hour, he contented himself with accompanying Lucius to the end of the street and then walking on to the station, there to await his coming.

He had to wait a good deal longer than he had

expected, and as the slow minute hand crept round the dial of the station clock his impatience increased to fever point. He had a good mind to go back to Marlow-street. What in heaven's name could Lucius have to say about that simple case of scarlatina which could not be said in a quarter of an hour? Ten minutes had been enough last night; to-day he had been more than an hour. Nine had struck on that slow-going station clock. The next up-train went at 9.15. Did Lucius mean to miss it, after all his talk about his London patients? As it was, he could not be in London till the afternoon. It seemed to Geoffrey as if this morning visit to the sick child was somewhat supercrogatory, since Lucius had declared the case to be one of the simplest.

Fretting himself thus he left the station, and on the windy high road between trim hedges, in which the hawthorn was sprouting greenly, and the little white flower-buds already began to show themselves, saw Lucius hurrying towards him at a sharp pace.

'I thought you meant to lose the next train,' said Geoffrey somewhat sharply. 'Well, what's your news?'

'The little girl has passed a very quiet night and is going on capitally, and you need have no farther alarm.'

'I didn't ask you about the little girl. You would hardly spend an hour talking about the scarlatina— Keep her cool, and give her the mixture regularly; and as soon as she is able to eat it let her have the wing of a chicken—as if one didn't know all that bosh. Why, you doctors rattle it off just as we used to say our Latin verbs at Winchester—*amo, amas, amat,* and so on. Of course, you have been talking about other things—drawing Mrs. Bertram out, I suppose? Come, Lucius, we've only five minutes. What did you think of her to-day?'

'The same as I thought last night. That she is a beautiful and noble woman, but that her past life has been overshadowed by some sad secret which we are never likely to know.'

'And you still warn me against her?'

'Still, with all my strength. Admire her, and respect her for all that is admirable in her nature, pity her for her misfortunes, but keep aloof.'

'Thanks for your remarkably disinterested advice,' said Geoffrey, with a bitter laugh. 'After devoting an hour of your precious time to this lady's society, you arrive at the conclusion that she is the last woman in the world for me. Yet you pay that child an unnecessary visit this morning in order to see the mother once more, and you come to me with a face as pale as—as the countenance of treachery itself.'

'Geoffrey!'

'However, as I don't mean to take your advice it makes very little difference. By the bye, here's your fee, Lucius; I promised Mrs. Bertram to see to that.' And he tried to thrust a folded cheque into the surgeon's hand.

This Lucius rejected with infinite scorn.

'What! you first ask my opinion, then call me a traitor because it happens not to jump with your own fancy, and then offer me money for a service for which you must know I could never dream of accepting payment. How utterly this foolish infatuation has changed you! But I have no time for discussion. Good-bye. There goes the bell, and I have to get my ticket.'

They ran into the station. Geoffrey, penitent already, stuck close to his friend until Lucius was seated in the second-class carriage which was to take him back to London and hard labour. Then he stretched out his hand.

'Shake hands, old fellow,' he said, with a remorseful look; 'of course I didn't mean anything; or only in a Pickwickian sense. Good-bye.'

The train bore off its burden and left Geoffrey stranded on the platform, perplexed, unhappy.

'I daresay he is right,' he said to himself, 'and I *know* that he is a good fellow. Yet why did he stay so long with her, and why did he look so pale and thoughtful when I met him?'

CHAPTER X.

A DAUGHTER'S LOVE, AND A LOVER'S HOPE.

Lucius Davoren's life had taken a new colour since that letter which opened the doors of the dismal old house in the Shadrack-road. His existence had now an object nearer to his human heart than even professional success. Dearly as he loved his profession, it is just possible that he loved himself a little better, and this new object, this new hope, concerned himself alone. Yet it did not in any manner distract him from his patient labours, from his indefatigable studies, but rather gave him a new incentive to industry. How better could he serve the interests of her whom he loved than by toiling steadily on upon the road which he believed must ultimately lead him to success, and even to fame—that far brighter reward than mere material prosperity?

Mr. Sivewright's condition had in no wise improved. That gradual decay had gone on a long time before the sturdy old man had cared to make his pains and languors known to any human being, much less to a member of that fraternity he affected to despise—the medical profession. All Lucius Davoren's care failed to bring back the vigour that had been wasted. He kept the feeble lamp of life burning, somewhat faintly, and that was all he could do yet awhile.

For some little time after the surgeon's admission to the house, Mr. Sivewright spent his evenings by the fireside in the parlour down-stairs. At Lucius's earnest request he had consented to the purchase of a more luxurious chair than the straight-backed instrument of torture in which he had been accustomed to sit. Here by the hearth, where a better fire burned than of old—for Lucius insisted that mistaken economy meant death—the bric-à-brac dealer sat and talked; talked of his youth, his bargains, his petty triumph over rival traders, but of that lost wanderer, his son, never.

'There must be something hard in a man's nature when even the approach of death does not soften his heart towards his own flesh and blood,' thought Lucius.

There came a time when the old man felt himself altogether too weak to leave his room. The broad shallow steps of the solid old staircase—so easy to the tread of youth and strength—became for him too painful a journey. He only left his bed to sit by the little bit of fire in his own room, or on warmer days by the open window.

This was some time after Lucius Davoren's visit to Stillmington, when spring had been succeeded by summer, which in the Shadrack-road district was distinguishable from the other seasons chiefly by an Egyptian plague of flies and an all-pervading atmosphere of dust; also by the shrill cries of costermongers vending cheap lots of gooseberries or periwinkles, and by an adoption of somewhat oriental or *al-fresco* habits among the population, who lounged at their doors, and stood about the streets a good deal in the long warm evenings, while respectable matrons did their domestic needlework seated on their doorsteps, whence they might watch their young barbarians at play in the adjacent gutter.

From this somewhat shabby and ragged out-of-door life on the king's highway, it was a relief for Lucius to enter the calm seclusion of the shadowy old house, where the June sunshine was tempered at midday by half-closed oaken shutters, and where it seemed to the surgeon there was ever a peculiar coolness and freshness, and faint perfume of some simple garden flower unknown elsewhere. In this sultry weather, when the outer world was as one vast oven, that sparsely-furnished parlour with its dark wainscot walls was a place to dream in; the dim old hall with its chaotic treasures saved from the wreck of time, a delicious retreat from the clamour and toil of life. Here Lucius loved to come, and here he was sure of a sweet welcome from her whom he had loved at first sight, and whom familiarity had made daily dearer to him.

Yes, he confessed now that the interest he had felt in Lucille Sivewright from the very first had its root in a deeper feeling than compassion. He was no longer ashamed to own that it was love, and love only, that had made yonder rusty iron gate, by which he had so often lingered, sad and longing, seem to him as the door of paradise.

One evening, after the old man had taken to his room up-stairs, and Lucille had been sorrowful and anxious, and had seemed in peculiar need of consolation, the old, old story was told once more under the pale stars of evening, as these two wandered about that patch of dusty sward above which the old cedar stretched his shrunken branches, and cast grim shadows on the shadowy grass. The creek with its black barges lay before them; beyond, a forest of roofs, and attic windows, and tall factory chimneys, and distant spars of mighty merchantmen faintly visible against the pale-gray sky. **Not a romantic spot, or a scene calculated to inspire the souls of lovers, by any means.** Yet Lucius was every whit as eloquent as he would have been had they wandered on the shores of Leman, or watched the sun go down **from the orange groves of Cintra.**

The girl heard him in profound silence. They had come to a pause in their desultory wanderings by the decaying ruin of an ancient summer-house, at an angle of the wall close to the creek—a spot which to the simpler tastes of untravelled citizens in the last century may have seemed eminently **picturesque.** Lucille sat **on** the broken **bench in a somewhat dejected attitude, her** arms resting on a battered **old table, her** face turned away from Lucius towards the dingy hulls that lay moored upon those muddy waters, unbeautiful as that dark ferry-boat which Dante saw advancing shadowy athwart the 'woeful tide of Acheron.'

He had spoken earnestly, and had pleaded well, but had been unable to read any answer in those truthful eyes, whose every expression he fancied he knew. Those had been **persistently averted from him.**

'Lucille, why do you turn from me ? My dearest, why this discouraging **silence ? Do** my words pain you? I had dared to hope they would not be unwelcome, that you must have expected to hear them. You must have known that I loved you, ever so long ago, for I have loved you from the very first.'

'You have been very good to me,' she said, in a low broken voice.

'Good to you!'

'So good that I have sometimes thought you—liked me a little.' (A woman's periphrasis; feminine lips hardly dare utter that mighty word 'love.') 'But if it is really so—which seems almost too much for me to believe' (if he could but have seen the proud happy look in her eyes as she said that!) —'I can only beg you never to say any more about it—until—'

'Until what, Lucille?' exclaimed Lucius impatiently. He had not expected to find hindrance or stumbling-block in the way of his happiness here. From Homer Sivewright there would no doubt be opposition, but surely not here. Had he so grossly deceived himself when he believed his love returned?

'Until my life is changed from what it is now, such a broken life, the merest fragment of a life,' answered Lucille quietly. 'How can I think of returning the affection you speak of—you so worthy to be loved—while I am in this miserable state of uncertainty about my father — not knowing if he is living or dead, fortunate or unhappy? I can never give my heart to any one, however noble'—with a lingering tenderness which might have told him that he was beloved—' until all doubts are cleared upon that one subject. Until then, I belong to my father. At any moment he might appear to claim me; and I am his'—with a passionate emphasis—' his, by the memory of that childhood, when I loved him so dearly. Let him order me to follow him to the other end of the world, and I should go—without one fear, without one regret.'

Lucius was silent for some moments, stung to the quick. Was a mere memory, the very shadow of her childhood's affection, so much nearer to her than his deep unselfish love—his love, which might brighten her dull life in the present, and open a fair vista of future happiness—that hopeful active love, which was to make a home for her, and win fame for him in the days to come, always for her sake?

'What, Lucille,' he said reproachfully, 'you hold my love so lightly that it can count for nothing when weighed against the memory of a father who deserted you—who has let all the years of your girlhood go by without making the faintest attempt to claim you, or even to see you?'

'How do I know what may have prevented him?' she asked—'what barrier may have stood between him and me? Death perhaps. He did not desert me.'

'Was not his sudden departure from your grandfather's house desertion of you?'

'No. He was driven away. I am very sure of that. My grandfather was hard and cruel to him.'

'Perhaps. But whatever quarrel may have parted those two, your claim on your father remained. You had not been hard or cruel; yet he abandoned you—tacitly renounced all claim upon you when he left his father's house. I don't want to blame him, Lucille; I don't want to spoil that idealised image which you carry in your heart; but surely it is not for you to sacrifice a very real affection in the present for a vague memory of the past.'

'It is not vague. My memory of those days is as vivid as my memory of yesterday—more vivid even. I have but to close my eyes—now, at this very moment while you are talking to me—and I can see my father's face; it is not your voice I hear, but his.'

'Infatuation, Lucille,' exclaimed the surgeon sadly. 'Had you known your father a few years longer, you might have discovered that he was utterly unworthy of your love—that fond confiding love of a child's guileless heart, prone to make for itself an idol.'

'If I had found him unworthy, I do not believe my love would have altered; I should only have been so much the more sorry for him. Remember, I am used to hear him badly spoken of. My grandfather's bitterest words have never lessened my love for him.'

'Granted that your love for him is indestructible, why should it stand between you and me—if I am not quite indifferent to you? Answer me that question first, Lucille; I am too much in earnest to be satisfied with half knowledge. Do you care for me, ever so little?'

She looked round at him for the first time, smiling, yet with tearful eyes—an expression that was half mournful, half arch.

'Ever so little,' she repeated. 'I might own to that. It does not commit me to much.'

'More than a little, then? O, be frank, Lucille! I have shown you all the weakness—or the strength —of *my* heart.'

'I love you very dearly,' she said shyly.

She was clasped to his breast before the words were half spoken, the kiss of betrothal pressed upon her trembling lips. She withdrew herself hastily from that first fond embrace.

'You have not heard half that I have to say, Mr. Davoren.'

'I will never consent to be Mr. Davoren again.'

'I will call you Lucius, then; only you must hear what I have to say. I do love you, very truly,' with a warning gesture that stopped any farther demonstration on his part; 'I do think you good and brave and noble. I am very proud to know that you care for me. But I can bind myself by no new tie until the mystery of my father's fate has been solved, until I am very sure that he will never claim my love and my obedience.'

'If I were to solve that mystery, Lucille—or at least attempt to solve it,' said Lucius thoughtfully.

'Ah, if! But you would never think of that! You could not spare time and thought for that; you have your profession.'

'Yes, and all my hopes of winning a position which might make you proud of being my wife by and by. It would be a hard thing to forego all those, Lucille—to devote my mind and my life to a perhaps hopeless endeavour. Fondly as I love you, I am not chivalrous enough to say I will shut up my surgery to-morrow and start on the first stage to the Antipodes, or the Japan Islands, or Heaven knows where, in quest of your father. Yet I might do something. If I had but the slightest foundation to work upon I should hardly be afraid of success. I would willingly do anything, anything less than the entire sacrifice of my prospects—which must be your prospects too, Lucille—to prove how dear you are to me.'

'You really would? Ah! if you could find him—if you could reunite us, I should love you so dearly—at least, no,' with a little gush of tenderness, 'I could not love you better than I do now. But you would make me so happy.'

'Then I will try, dearest, try honestly. But if I fail—after earnest endeavour, and at the end of a reasonable period—if I fail in bringing your father to you living, or discovering when and how he died, you will not punish me for my failure. You will be my wife two or three years hence, come what may, Lucille. Give me that hope, sweet one. It will make me strong enough to face all difficulties.'

'I love you,' she said in her low serious voice, putting her little hand into his; and that simple admission he accepted as a promise.

CHAPTER XI.

THE BIOGRAPHY OF A SCOUNDREL.

The weakness and the languor that kept Homer Sivewright a prisoner in his bedroom were not the tokens of mortal illness. Death kept as yet at a respectful distance. The patient's life might be prolonged even to man's appointed measure of three score and ten, with care and skilful treatment. There was organic disease, but of a mild type. Lucius was not without hopes of a rally—that a period of perfect repose and quiet might, in some measure, restore the enfeebled frame—which, gaunt and wasted by sickness, was yet so mighty a skeleton. The man was tough; a creature of strong fibres, and muscles that had once been like iron. Above all, his life had been strictly temperate. Lucius augured well from these facts. The disease would remain always, more or less subject to treatment, but there might be a partial recovery.

'You need not be anxious,' he said, when Lucille questioned him earnestly about her grandfather. 'Mr. Sivewright will be a long time dying. Or, in other words, he will fight hard with Death. We may keep him alive for some years longer, Lucille, **if we take trouble.**'

'I shall **not think** anything a trouble. I do **not** forget how good he has **been to me, in** his own cold way. But he has seemed so much weaker lately.'

'Only because he has at last consented to succumb **to Nature.** He would not before admit, even **to him-self,** that he is an old man. Nature counselled him **to** rest, but it pleased him better to go on labouring, and, as it were, pretending to be still young. He has given in at last; and Nature, **the** great restorer, may **do** much for him, always assisted by careful nursing— and I think you are **the best nurse I ever met with,** Lucille.'

'I have not much experience, but **I do my best.**'

'And your best is better than other people's. You **have** the soft low voice, the gentle footstep, which make a woman's help precious in a sick-room. **Don't** be anxious about your grandfather, dearest. We shall **pull him** through, rely **upon it.**'

There was that **in his** protecting tone, the fond **look in the** grave eyes, which told how secure the lover felt, despite that hard condition wherewith Lucille had hampered the promise of her love. Thus time went on in the dull old house, which to these two was not all gloomy—which to one at least was full of hope and pleasant thoughts, and bright dreams of a fair life to come.

Propriety, as known in what is called society, had no bondage for these lovers. In their lives there was actually no Mrs. Grundy; not even a next-door neighbour of the maiden-lady persuasion to keep count of Mr. Davoren's visits, and to wonder what old Mr. Sivewright meant by allowing such an outrage of the proprieties under his very nose. Lucius came and went as he pleased, stayed as long as he liked, within reasonable limits. He read Shakespeare to Lucille in the summer gloaming; he poured out all the wealth of his mind to her in long conversations that were almost monologues, the girl eager to learn, he eager to teach; or rather to make the woman he loved a sharer in all his thoughts, fancies, creeds, and dreams—verily the better and purer half of himself. At other times they wandered about the bare old garden together, or sat in the ruined summer-house; and happy in that complete and perfect universe which they possessed in each other, forgot that the mud-bespattered wharf was not the Rialto, the slimy water that stagnated beneath the barges something less lovely than the Adriatic's sunlit blue.

They talk much of the future, after the manner of lovers. Although they were so completely happy in each other's company, and in that calm security which blesses innocent reciprocal love, this little spot of time, the present, counted for nothing in their scheme of life. It may be said that they were happy without being aware of their happiness. And this is true of many lives. The one happy hour in the long dull life slips by unnoted, like water-drops running between one's fingers. And then years after—when, remembering that brief glimpse of paradise, we look back and would fain return to that green spot beside life's long dusty beaten turnpike-road—the grass is withered, or the Commons Enclosure Act has swallowed up our pleasant resting-place: or where Poetry's fairy palace shone radiant in youth's morning sunlight, there is now only the cold marble of a Tomb.

Lucius and Lucille talked of their future—the fame that he was to win, the good that he was to do; noble schemes for the welfare of others, to be realised when fame and wealth were gained; cottage hospitals in pleasant suburban spots, near enough at hand for the sick or worn-out Londoner, and yet with green fields and old trees and song birds about them ; chosen retreats where the country yet lingered ; little bits of rustic landscape over which the enterprising builder had not yet spread his lime-whitened paw ; meadows whose hawthorn hedges were undefiled by smoke, across whose buttercups and crimson sorrel-flowers no speculative eye had yet ranged with a view to ground rents.

The young surgeon had various schemes for the improvement of his fellow creatures' condition—some wholly philanthropic, others scientific. To all Lucille listened with the same eager interest, worshipping him in her loving womanly way, as if he had been as wise as Socrates. After that first confession of her love, wrung from unwilling lips, there had been no more reserve. She made no mystery of her affection, which was childlike in its simple reverence for those lofty qualities that women are apt to perceive in the object of their regard some time before the rest of the world has awakened to a sense thereof. But she held firmly by the condition which she had imposed on her lover. She would never be his wife, she would begin no new stage of existence, until the mystery of her father's fate had been solved.

The time had now come when Lucius deemed it a point of honour to inform Mr. Sivewright of this engagement, but not of the condition attaching thereto. He had not forgotten what the old man had said in the first instance, 'My granddaughter is disposed of;' but this he imagined was only an idle threat. Day by day he found himself more necessary to the invalid. Mr. Sivewright looked anxiously for his visits, detained him as long as it was possible for him to stay, would have him come back in the evening to sit for an hour or so in the sick-room, talking, or reading the day's news to him; proved himself, in fact, the most exacting of patients. But in all their intercourse he had expressed no dislike to that intimacy between Lucius and Lucille which he must needs have been aware of; since he saw them together daily, and must have been blind if he failed to see that they were something nearer and dearer to each other than common friends.

'He cannot be very much surprised when he hears the truth,' thought Lucius, and only deferred his confession until he perceived a marked improvement in his patient.

This arose a little later in the summer, when the old man was able to come down-stairs again, now and then, and even creep about the dreary waste he called his garden.

One evening, in the very spot where he had first

told his love to Lucille, Lucius mustered courage and took Mr. Sivewright into his confidence, only reserving that hard condition which Lucille had attached to her promise.

The old man received this communication with a cynical grin.

'Of course,' he said, 'I have seen it all along. As if one ever could trust a young man and a young woman to play at being brother and sister without their exchanging that sentimental make-believe for the reality of love-making! Well, I am not angry. I told you my granddaughter was disposed of. That was true so far as it went. I had views for her; but they were vague, and hinged upon my own health and vigour. I thought I had a stronger part to play in life's drama. Well,' with a faint sigh, 'I can afford to resign those old hopes. You may marry Lucille, whenever you can afford to keep her in comfort and respectability. Now, my dear Mr. Davoren,' turning to the surgeon with a look of infinite cunning in his keen eyes, 'I daresay you think you have made a lucky hit—that, in spite of all I have told you, this show of poverty is only a miser's pretence: that I have railway shares and consols and debentures and Heaven knows what in my shabby old desk, and that I shall die worth half-a-million. Dismiss that delusion from your mind at once and for ever. If you take Lucille Sivewright for your wife you take a pauper. My collection is all I possess: and I shall leave that most likely to a museum.'

Thus ungraciously did Mr. Sivewright receive Lucius into the bosom of his family. Yet, in his own eccentric fashion, he seemed attached to the young man; courted his society, and had evidently an exalted belief in his honour.

Nothing had Lucius yet done towards even the beginning of that endeavour to which he had pledged himself; but he had thought deeply and constantly of the task that had been imposed upon him, and had tried to see his way to its accomplishment.

Given a man who had been missing twelve years, who in person, profession, and surroundings was utterly unknown to him, and who had cut every tie that bound him to kindred or home; who might be in any quarter of the globe, or in his grave—and how to set about the work of finding him? That was the problem which Lucille had proposed to him as calmly as if it were the simplest thing in the world.

A very little consideration showed him that his only hope lay in beginning his investigation close at home. Unless he could obtain certain details from the old man—unless he could overcome Homer

Sivewright's objection to the subject, and induce him to talk freely about his missing son—the case seemed beyond all measure hopeless. And even if the father could be made to speak, even if Lucius could learn all that was to be told of Ferdinand Sivewright's history at the time he left his home in Bond-street, there would be still a dreary gulf of twelve years to be bridged over.

To question the old man was, however, the easiest and most obvious course. He might or might not remain obstinately dumb.

One morning, when the patient's case seemed more than usually promising—pain banished, and something of his old strength regained—Lucius made his first approach to this difficult subject.

Their conversation, which was apt to wander widely, from the sordid business of life to the loftiest regions of metaphysical speculation, had on this occasion drifted into a discussion of the Christian faith.

Mr. Sivewright contemplated that mighty theme from a purely critical standpoint; talked of the Gospel as he talked of the *Iliad;* admitted this and denied that; brought the hard dry logic of an unpoetical mind, the narrow scepticism of a suspicious nature, to bear upon divine truths. Lucius spoke with the quiet conviction of a man who believed and was not ashamed to stand **to his colours.** From a theological argument he led the old man to the question **of** Christian charity, as distinguished from mere Pagan humanitarianism; and here he found his opportunity.

'I have often wondered,' he said, 'that you—**who seem in most things a man of a calm temperament, even if** somewhat stern—should yet cherish a lifelong anger against an only son. Forgive me for touching upon a subject **which I know is painful to** you—'

'It is not painful,' answered Sivewright sharply; 'no more painful than if you **spoke to me of any** scoundrel in the next street whose face I had never **seen.** Do you think that hearts are everlasting wear? There was a time when to think of my false, ungrateful guilty son was like the smart of a gun-shot wound. But that was years ago. All the tissues of my body have been changed since he deserted me. **Do you** suppose **that regret** and affection and shame, and the sense of kinship, do not wear out as well **as** flesh and **blood?** Twelve years ago Homer Sivewright lamented the only son who had disgraced him. I, the man who speaks to you to-day,' touching his breast with his lean hand, 'have no son.'

'A hard saying,' replied Lucius compassionately,

for there was more real feeling in this man's assumed coldness than in many a loud-spoken and demonstrative grief; 'yet I can but believe—unworthy as he may have seemed to you—he still holds a corner in your heart.'

A cloud came over the keen eyes, the gray head drooped, but Homer Sivewright made no admission of weakness.

'Seemed unworthy,' he repeated; 'he *was* unworthy.'

'You have never told me his crime.'

The old man lifted his head, and looked at the speaker with those penetrating eyes of his, for an instant resentfully, then with the cynicism which was his second nature.

'What, are you curious?' he said. 'Well, I suppose you have a right to know something of the family you propose to honour with your alliance. Know, then, that the father of your intended wife was a liar and a thief.'

Lucius recoiled as if some outrageous insult had been offered to himself.

'I cannot believe—' he began.

'Wait till you have heard the story before you attempt to dispute the facts. You know what my youth was—laborious, self-denying. I married early, but my marriage was a disappointment. I made the somewhat common error of taking a handsome face as a certificate of womanly excellence. My wife was a Spanish American, with a face like an old Italian picture. Unhappily, she had a temper which made her own life a burden, and produced a corresponding effect upon the lives of other people. She had an infinite capacity for discontent. She could be spasmodically gay under the influence of what is called pleasure, but happy never. Had I been monarch of the world, I doubt if I could have ever gratified half her wishes, or charmed the sullen demon in her breast. She rarely desired anything that was not unattainable. Judge, then, how she endured the only kind of existence I could offer her.

'I did all in my power to make her life pleasant, or at least tolerable. As my means improved I gave her the command of money; bought birds and flowers for her sitting-room, and furnished it with my choicest buhl cabinets, my prettiest Louis-Seize sofa, the spoil of French palaces; but she laughed to scorn my attempts to beautify a home above a shop. Her father —a planter, and when I married her a bankrupt— had once been rich. The days of his prosperity had scarcely outlasted her childhood, but they had lasted long enough to accustom her to habits of recklessness and extravagance which no after experience could eradicate. I soon found that to give her freedom in money matters would be to accomplish my own ruin. From an indulgent husband I became what she called a miserly tyrant. Passive discontent now changed to active aversion; and she began a series of quarrels which, on more than one occasion, ended in her running away from home, and taking refuge with a distant relation of her mother's—a frivolous extravagant widow whom I detested. I followed and brought her back from these flights; but she returned unwillingly, and each occasion widened the breach.

'Our child made no link between us. When the boy grew old enough to take any part in our quarrels, he invariably sided with his mother. Naturally enough, since he was always with her, heard her complaints of my ill-usage, was indulged by her with wanton folly, and gratified with pleasures that were paid for with money stolen from me. Yes, that was the beginning of his unprincipled career. The mother taught her son to plunder my cash-box or my till.'

'Very horrible!' said Lucius.

'Even to him, however,' continued Mr. Sivewright, who, having once drifted into the story of his domestic wrongs, waxed garrulous, 'even to him she was violent; and I discovered ere long that there was often ill-blood between them. Taunts, innuendoes, sneers, diversified the sullen calm of our wretched hearth; and one day the boy, Ferdinand, came to me and entreated me to send him to school; he could not endure life with his mother any longer. "Why, I thought you doated on her," said I. "I am fond enough of *her*," he answered, "but I can't stand her temper. You'd better send me to school, father, or something unpleasant may happen. I threw a knife at her after dinner yesterday. You remember what you told me about that Roman fellow whose head you showed me on a coin the other day—the man who murdered his mother. I'm not likely to go in for the business in his cold-blooded way; but if she goes on provoking me as she does sometimes, I may be goaded into stabbing her."

'He wound up this cool avowal by informing me that he would like to complete his education in Germany. He was at this time about twelve.'

'You complied, I suppose?' suggested Lucius.

'Not entirely. I wished my son to be an English gentleman. I wanted, if possible, to eradicate the South American element, which had already exhibited itself in violent passions and an inordinate love of pleasure. One talent, and one only, he had displayed to any great extent; and that was a talent, or, as his mother and her few friends declared, a genius for music. From five years old his chief delight was scraping a fiddle or strumming on his mother's piano. Now, for my own part,' added Mr. Sivewright candidly, 'I hate music.'

'And I have loved it,' said Lucius thoughtfully. 'Yet it is strange that the darkest memories of my life are associated with music.'

'I didn't want the son for whom I had toiled, and was willing to go on toiling for the rest of my days, to become a fiddler. I told him as much in the plainest words, and sent him to a private tutor; in that manner beginning an education which was to cost me as much as if I had been a man of wealth and position. I hoped that education might cure the vices of his childhood, and make him a good man. From the tutor he went to Harrow, from Harrow to Oxford, your own college, Balliol. But before this period of his life his mother ran away from me for the last time. I declined to go through the usual business of bringing her home again, but gave her a small allowance and requested her to remain away. She stayed with the South American widow in Thistle-grove; spent her allowance, I fear, chiefly upon brandy, and died in less than a year after she left me. My son went to see her when she was dying; heard her last **counsel, which** doubtless advised him to hate me; and went back to Harrow, a boy, with the passions of **a man.**'

There was a pause, and once more the old man's chin sunk upon his breast, the cold gray eyes fixed themselves **with that** far-off **gaze which sees the** things that **are no more. Then** rousing himself with an impatient sigh **he went on.**

'**I needn't** trouble you with the details of his University life. Enough that he contrived to make it an epitome of the vices. He assented sullenly **to** adopt a profession — **the law; skulked; spent his** days and **nights in** dissipation ; **wasted my money ;** and compelled me at last to say, " **Shut up your** books, if **you have ever opened them.** Nature never meant **you for a lawyer. But you** have all the sharpness of your mother's **wily** race. Come home, and in **my** petty business learn the science **of commerce. You** may be a **great merchant by and by.**"'

'You must have loved **him in those days, or** you would hardly have been so lenient,' said Lucius.

'Loved **him, yes,**' answered **the other, with a** long regretful sigh. '**I** loved him and was proud of him ; proud in spite of his vices ; proud of his good looks, his cleverness, his plausible tongue—the tongue that **lied to me and swindled me. God** help me, he was the only thing I had to love! He came home, pretended to take to the business. Never was a man better qualified to prosper in such a trade. He had a keen appreciation of art; was quick at learning the jargon which deludes amateur buyers; and in the business of bargain-driving would have Jewed the veriest Jew alive. But his habits were against anything like sustained industry. It was not till after he had won my confidence, and wheedled me into giving him a partnership, that I discovered how little he had changed his old ways. As he had robbed me before he was twelve years old, so he robbed me now; only as his necessities were larger, I felt his dishonesty more. I saw my stock shrinking, my books doctored. Vainly I tried to battle with an intellect that was stronger than my own. Long after I knew him to be a rogue, he was able to demonstrate to me, by what seemed the soundest logic, that I was mistaken. One day, when he had been living with me something more than a year, he informed me, in his easy-going way, that he had married some years before, lost his wife soon after, and that I was a grandfather. "You're fond of children," he said. "I've seen you notice those little curly-headed beggars next door. You'd better let me send for Lucille."'

'You consented?'

'Of course. **Lucille came the** same night. A pale melancholy child, in whose small face I **saw no** likeness to any of my race. Of her mother I could ascertain very little. **My** son was reticent. His wife was of decent birth, he said, and had possessed a little money, which he had spent, and that was all he ever **told me.** Of how or where she died, he said nothing. Lucille **talked of green** fields and flowers and the sea; but knew no more of the whereabouts of her previous home than if she had come straight **from Paradise.**'

'Then you do not even know her mother's maiden-name?'

'**No.** That's hard upon you, isn't it? There'll be a blank in your children's pedigree.'

'I will **submit** to the blank; only it seems rather hard upon Lucille that she should never have known her mother's relatives, that she should have been cheated of any affection they might have given her.'

'Affection! the affection of aunts and uncles and **cousins!** Milk-and-water!'

'**Well, sir, you and your son contrived to live to-**gether for some years.'

'Yes, it lasted a long time—I 'knowing I was cheated, yet unable to prove it; he spending his days in sloth, his nights in dissipation, yet every now and then, by some brilliant stroke of business, compelling me to admire him. My customers liked him, the young men especially; for he had all those modern ideas which were as strange to me as a Cuneiform inscription. Somehow he brought grist to the mill. His University friends found him out, made my shop a lounge, borrowed my money, and paid me a protective rate of interest. We had our quarrels—not violent and noisy, like the quarrels in which women are concerned, but perhaps all the more lasting in their effect. Where he went at night I knew not, until going into his room very early one morning to wake him—there was to be a great picture-sale twenty miles from London that day, and I wanted him to attend it—I saw some gold and notes scattered on the table by his bedside. From that moment I knew the worst of his vices. He was a gambler. Where he played or with whom I never knew. I never played the spy upon him, or attempted to get at his secrets in any underhand manner. One day I taxed him with this vice. He shrugged his shoulders, and affected supreme candour. "I play a little sometimes," he said—"games of skill, not chance. It is impossible to keep such company as I keep and not take an occasional hand at whist or écarté. And you ought not to forget that my friends have been profitable to you."

A year after this I had occasion to sell a portion of my stock at Christie's, in order to obtain ready money to purchase the lease of premises adjoining my own—premises which would enable me to enlarge my art gallery. The things were sold, and, a few days afterwards, settled for. I brought home the money—between five and six hundred pounds—locked it in my safe, impregnable even to my junior partner, and sat down to dinner with the key in my pocket, and, as I believed, my money secure.'

Again there was a pause, painful recollections contracting the deeply-lined brow, gloomy thoughts clouding the eyes.

'Well, I had come home late; the child was in bed, and my son and I dined together by the fire in the little parlour behind the shop—my wife's fine drawing-room had been absorbed long ago into the art gallery. Never had Ferdinand been so genial or so gay. He was full of talk about the extension of our premises; discussed our chances of success like a thorough man of business. We had a bottle of good old burgundy in honour of our brilliant prospects. I did not drink more than usual; yet half an hour after dinner I was in the deepest sleep that ever stole my senses, and reduced me to the condition of a lifeless log. In a word, the wine had been drugged, and by the hand of my son. When I awoke it was long after midnight, the hearth was black and cold, the candles had burned down to the sockets. I woke with a violent headache, and that nausea which is the after-taste of opium or morphine. I sat for some minutes shivering, and wondering what was the matter with me. Almost mechanically I felt in my pocket for the key of the safe. Yes, there it lay, snug enough. I staggered up to bed, surprised at the unusual effect of a couple of glasses of burgundy, and was so ill next morning that my old housekeeper sent for the nearest apothecary. He felt my pulse, looked at my eyes, and asked if I had taken an opiate. Then it flashed upon me in a moment that I had been drugged. The instant the apothecary left me I got out of bed, dragged on my clothes, and went down to examine my safe. The money was gone. Ferdinand knew when I was to receive the cash, and knew my habits well enough to know where I should put it, careful as I had been not to let him see me dispose of it. I had been robbed—dexterously—by my own son.'

'Scoundrel!' muttered Lucius.

'Yes. I might have stomached the theft; I couldn't forgive the opiate. That stung me to the quick. A man who would do that would poison me, I thought; and I plucked my only son out of my heart, as you drag up a foul weed whose roots have gone deep and have a tough hold in a clay soil. It was a wrench, and left a feeling of soreness for after years; but I think my love for him died in that hour. Could one love so paltry a villain? I made no attempt to pursue him, nor to regain my money. One can hardly deliver one's own flesh and blood to the tender mercies of the criminal code.'

'You never told his daughter?'

'No; I was not cruel enough for that. I did my best to impress upon her mind that he was unworthy of affection or regret, without stating the nature of his offence. Unhappily, with her romantic temperament, to be unfortunate is to be worthy of compassion. I know that she has wept for him and regretted him, and even set up his image in her heart, in spite of me.'

'How much do you know of your son's fate?'

'Almost nothing. By mere accident I heard that he went to America within a month of the day on which he robbed me. More than that I never heard.'

'Do you remember the name of the ship—or steamer—in which he went?'

'That's a curious question; however, I don't

mind answering it. He went in a Spanish sailing-ship, El Dorado, bound for Rio.'

This was all—a poor clue wherewith to discover the whereabouts of a man who had been missing twelve years.

CHAPTER XII.

LUCIUS HAS AN INTERVIEW WITH A FAMOUS PERSONAGE.

It is one thing for a man to make a rash promise, but another thing for him to keep it. A man in love will pledge himself to any enterprise—to any adventure—even to the discovery of a new planet or a new continent, should his mistress demand as much. After contemplating the question from every possible point of view, Lucius Davoren was disposed to think that he had pledged himself to the performance of something that was more impossible than astronomical or geographical discovery, when he promised to find Lucille Sivewright's father, or, failing that, obtain for her at least the story of his fate.

It had seemed a great point to get the old man to speak freely of his lost son; but even with this new light thrown upon the business, an Egyptian darkness still surrounded the figure of the missing man. He had sailed for a certain port. He might be still a denizen of that Southern city. Yet what less likely in such a man's career than continued residence anywhere? The criminal is naturally a wanderer. He has no fixed abiding-place. Fresh woods and pastures new are the necessity of his contraband existence. Like a smuggled keg of cognac, he passes from place to place under a cloud of mystery. None see him arrive or depart. Like the chamelion, he changes colour — now wearing dyed whiskers and a wig, now returning to the hues of nature. He has as many names as the Roman Jupiter.

Had Lucius been a free man, he might have gone straight to Rio, and hunted up the traces of the missing man, unaided and alone. He might have discovered some clue even after the lapse of years since the sailing of the Spanish merchantman El Dorado. It was just within the limits of possibility that he might have found the man himself.

But to do this would have involved the abandonment of much that was of vital moment to himself— would have indeed thrown the whole scheme of his existence out of gear. In the first place he was poor, and his pitiful salary as parish doctor was of inestimable value to him. Now, a parish doctor has no more liberty to rove than the parish turncock, and vast would be the wonder of the vestry—or the overseers

—if informed that the parish surgeon had gone for a fortnight's grouse shooting on the Sutherland hills, or set sail for the Mediterranean in a friend's yacht, or joined one of the great Cook's caravans bound for Egypt or Peru.

Again, Lucius had now the nucleus of a very fair private practice. His patients, for the most part small tradesmen, paid punctually, and there were among them some wealthy traders whose custom was worth having. He saw the beginning, very small it is true, but the beginning of fortune. That dream of Savile-row was to be realised out of such small beginnings. His patients believed in him, and talked of him; and so far as reputation can be made in such a place as the Shadrack-Basin district, his reputation was fast being made. To turn his back upon all this would be to sacrifice, or at any rate to postpone indefinitely, his hope of winning a home for the woman he loved.

Beyond this there remained a third reason why he should refrain from setting forth upon that wild-goose chase which, however barren as to result, would at least serve to prove him the most devoted and chivalrous of lovers. To go to Rio was to leave Lucille, and for an indefinite period; since the business upon which he would go was essentially a business requiring deliberation, ample leisure, time for inquiry, for travelling to and fro, time enough to waste in following up trails which, though promising much, might prove false,—time and indomitable patience. How could he afford time and patience with his heart racked by fears for the safety of Lucille? What might not happen during his absence? The old man was in so precarious a condition that his illness might at any moment take a fatal turn—in a state so critical that to deliver him over to a strange doctor, and perhaps a careless one, would be a kind of assassination.

Thus, after profound thought, Lucius determined that even love should not impel him to so rash a course as a voyage to Rio in quest of Ferdinand Sivewright.

'After all,' he said to himself, 'there is no wiser saying than that of Apelles to the cobbler, "Let every man stick to his own trade." I may be a clever surgeon, but a very poor detective-officer; and it will be safer to spend the little money I can spare in employing a retired policeman than in trying my 'prentice hand in the art of detection. We bluster a good deal in the newspapers about the incompetence of the police, when they fail to hunt up a criminal who has plunged into the great sea of humanity, leaving not a bubble to mark the place where he went down; yet I doubt if any of those brilliant journalists who furnish indignant editorials on the police question would do much better in the detective line than the officials whose failures they ridicule. Yes, I will submit the case to Mr. Otranto, the private detective.'

Once resolved, Lucius lost no more time; but called at Mr. Otranto's office in the city, and was fortunate enough to find that gentleman at home—a plain-mannered little man, with a black frock-coat buttoned up to the chin, and the half-military stamp of the ex-policeman strong upon him. He was a brisk little man, too, disinclined to waste time upon unnecessary detail.

To him Lucius freely confided all he knew about Ferdinand Sivewright—his character, antecedents, the ship in which he sailed, the port from which he went, the approximate date of his departure.

Mr. Otranto shrugged his shoulders. He had whistled a little impromptu accompaniment to Mr. Davoren's statement under his breath; a kind of internal whistling, indicative of deepest thought.

'I'm afraid it's not the most hopeful case,' he said; 'twelve years is a long time. See what a number of earthquakes and shipwrecks and revolutions and what you may call general blow-ups you get in a dozen years; and then consider the case of one individual man who may drop through at any moment, who, being by nature a bad lot, will change his name any number of times. However, I can put the business into the hands of a party out yonder who will do all that can be done on the spot.'

'Yonder, meaning Rio?' inquired Lucius. 'Have you correspondents so far afield?'

'Sir,' said Mr. Otranto, with a complacent glance at the map of the world which hung against the wall opposite him, 'there are very few corners of this habitable earth where I have *not* a correspondent.'

The business was settled without farther discussion. Lucius gave Mr. Otranto a substantial deposit, to prove that his inquiry was not prompted by frivolity, and to insure that gentleman's zeal; private inquiry being, as Mr. Otranto indirectly informed his client, a somewhat expensive luxury.

This done, Lucius felt that he had not been false to his pledge. He told Lucille nothing, however, except that he meant to keep his promise, so far as it was possible and reasonable for him to keep it.

'If I tell you that I think you foolish for cherishing a wild hope, dearest, you will tell me that I am unkind,' he said, as they paced their favourite walk in the barren old garden at sunset that evening.

'Lucius,' asked Lucille, not long after this, 'I am going to ask you a favour.'

'My dearest, what do **I live** for except to please you?'

'O, Lucius, a great many things; for your patients, for science, for the **hope of** being a famous **doctor** by and **by.**'

'Only secondary objects in my life now, **Lucille.** They once made the sum of life, I grant; they **are** henceforth **no more** than means to an end—and that end is the creation of a home for you.'

'How good of you to say that! I am hardly worthy of such love, when my heart dwells so much upon the past. Yet, Lucius, if you could only **know** how I cling to the memory of that dim strange time, which seems almost as far away as a dream, you would forgive me even for putting that memory above my affection for you.'

'**I forgive you** freely, darling, for a sentiment which does but prove the tenderness and constancy of your nature. I am content even to hold the second place. But what is the favour you have to ask, **Lucille?**'

'Let me hear you play. Poor grandpapa is seldom down-stairs of an evening now. There could be **no harm in** your bringing your violin, and playing a little now and then when he has gone back to his **room.** His room is so far from the parlour that **he** would never hear you; and, after all, playing the violin is not a crime. Do let me hear you, Lucius! The old sweet sad music will remind me of my father. And I know you play divinely,' she added, looking up at him with innocent admiring eyes.

What could he do? He was mortal, loved music to distraction, and had some belief in his own playing.

'So be it, my weestest. I'll bring the Amati; but you must stow him away in some dusky corner between whiles, where your grandfather cannot possibly discover him, or he might wreak his vengeance upon my treasure. After all, as you say, there can be no harm in a violin, and it will be hardly a breach of honour for me to play you a sonata now and then, after my patient has gone to bed. Your father must have been a fine player, or his playing would have hardly made such an impression upon you as a child of seven.'

'Yes,' she answered dreamily, 'I suppose it was what you call fine playing. I know that it was sometimes mournful as the cry of a broken heart, sometimes wild and strange—so strange that it has made me cling closer to his knees, as I sat at his feet in the dusky room, afraid to look round lest I should see some unearthly form conjured out of the shadows by that awful music. You know how children look behind them with scared faces as they cower round the Christmas fire, listening to a ghost story. I have felt like that when I listened to my father's playing.'

'I will bring you pleasanter music, Lucille, and conjure no ghosts out of the evening shadows—only happy thoughts of our future.'

This was the prelude to many peaceful evenings, full of a placid happiness which knew not satiety. Lucius brought his Amati, feeling very much like a conspirator when he conveyed the instrument into Mr. Sivewright's house by stealth, as it were, and gave it into Lucille's keeping, to be hidden by day, and only to be brought forth at night, when her grandfather had retired to his remote bedchamber, beyond ken of those sweet sounds.

The old woman in the bonnet—who was at once housekeeper, cook, laundress, and parlour-maid in this curious establishment — was of course in the secret. But Lucius had found this ancient female improve upon acquaintance, and he was now upon intimate and friendly terms with her. She had lived for an indefinite length of years in Mr. Sivewright's service—remembered Lucille's childhood in the dark old back rooms in Bond-street — but no power of persuasion could extract any information from her.

Upon entering Mr. Sivewright's household in the remote past she had promised to hold her tongue; and she was religiously silent to this hour. Of the old man she could never be induced to say more than that he was a 'carrack-ter;' a remark which, accompanied as it always was with a solemn shake of her head, might be complimentary or otherwise.

Lucille she praised with fondest enthusiam, but of Lucille's father she said not a word. On the various occasions when Lucius had ventured to press his questions on this subject, she had acted always in the same manner. Her countenance assumed a dark and forbidding aspect; she abruptly set down the dish, or tray, or teapot, or whatever object she might happen to be carrying, and as abruptly vanished from the room. Persistence here availed nothing.

'Mr. Sivewright bound me over not to talk about his business when he first engaged me,' she said once, when hard pressed by Lucius, who had hoped through her to obtain some better clue to the fate of Ferdinand Sivewright. 'I've held my tongue for uppards o' five-and-twenty years. It ain't likely I should begin to blab now.'

Although uncommunicative, this faithful domestic was not unfriendly. She treated Lucille with an affectionate familiarity, and in a manner took the lovers under her wing.

'I was sure and certain, the first time I laid eyes on him, that you and Dr. Davory would keep company,' she said to Lucille; and her protecting influence overshadowed the lovers at all times, like the wings of a guardian angel. She evidently regarded herself in the light of Miss Sivewright's duenna; and would come away from some mysterious operations in the labyrinthine offices and outhouses of the ancient mansion, where she had a piece of lumber which she spoke of casually as her good gentleman, in order to hover about Lucille and Lucius in their walks, or to listen, awestricken and open-mouthed, to the strains of the violin. Discovering ere long that this rough unpolished jewel was not wanting in some of the finer qualities of the diamond, Lucius admitted Mrs. Wincher, in some measure, to his confidence—discussed his future freely in her presence, imparted his hopes and fears, and felt that perhaps within this unbeauteous husk dwelt the soul of a friend; and assuredly neither he nor Lucille could afford to sacrifice a friend on account of external shortcomings. So Mrs. Wincher was accepted by him, bonnet and all, and her hoverings about the pathway of innocent love went unreproved.

'I am so glad you are not angry with Wincher for being a little too familiar,' said Lucille. 'She cannot forget that she took care of me when I was a poor solitary child in those back rooms in Bond-street; and I know she is faithful and good.'

Jacob Wincher, or Mrs. Wincher's good gentleman, was a feeble prowling old man, who took charge of the collection, and pottered about from morn till dewy eve—which, by the way, never was dewy in the Shadrack district—dusting, polishing, arranging, and rearranging Mr. Sivewright's treasures—a very feeble old man, but learned in all the mysteries of bric-à-brac, and enthusiastic withal; a man whose skilful hands wandered about among egg-shell china, light as the wings of a butterfly. He had been Mr. Sivewright's factotum in Bond-street, but was no more inclined to be communicative than Mrs. Wincher, whom he spoke of, with reciprocal respect, as his good lady.

Happy summer evenings, when, in the deepening dusk, Lucius awoke the sweet sad strains of his violin, while Lucille sat knitting by the window, and Mrs. Wincher, in the inevitable bonnet, occupied the extreme edge of a chair by the door, listening with folded arms and the serious attention of a musical critic.

'I can't say but what I've a preference for livelier toons,' she would remark, after patiently awaiting the end of a dirge by Spohr, 'but the fingering is beautiful. I like to watch the fingering. My good gentleman used to play the fiddle very sweet afore we was married—"John Anderson my Jones," and the "Bird Waltz," and "British Grenayders," and such-like—but he give it up afterwards. There was no time to waste upon music in Bond-street. Up early and abed late, and very often travel a hundred miles backards and forrards between morning and night to attend a sale in the country—that was Mr. Sivewright's motter.'

These musical entertainments were naturally of rare occurrence. Mr. Sivewright had been for some time gradually improving, and was more inclined for society as his strength returned, but was, on the other hand, disinclined to come down-stairs; so Lucius and Lucille had to spend the greater part of their time in his room, where Lucius entertained his patient with tidings of the outer world, while Lucille made tea at a little table in the narrow space which the collector had left clear in the midst of his crowded chamber. There were a few flowers now in the one unobstructed window, and Lucille had done all she could, with her small means, to make the room pretty and homelike.

Mr. Sivewright listened while the lovers discussed their future, but with no indulgent ear.

'Love and poverty!' he said, with his harsh laugh; 'a nice stock-in-trade upon which to set up in the business of life! However, I suppose you are no more foolish than all the fools who have travelled the same beaten road before your time: and the same old question remains to be solved by you, just as it has been solved by others —whether the love will outwear the poverty, or the poverty wear out the love.'

'We are not afraid to stand the test,' said Lucius.

'We are not afraid,' echoed Lucille.

CHAPTER XIII.

HE FEARS HIS FATE TOO MUCH.

THE quiet course of Lucius Davoren's life, so full of hard work and high hopes and simple unalloyed happiness, was by and by interrupted by a summons from Geoffrey, that spoiled child of fortune, who, in his hour of perplexity, turned again to that staunch friend whose counsel he had set at naught.

This was Geoffrey Hossack's letter:

'Stillmington, August 13th.

'Dear Lucius,—I daresay you'll be surprised to see me still abiding in this sleepy old place, when yesterday's gray dawn saw the first shot fired on many a moor from York to Inverness. However, here I am, and in sore distress of mind, no nearer a hopeful issue out of my perplexities than I was when you ran down here nearly four months ago to see that dear child. Will you come down again, like a good old fellow, forget how rude and ungracious I was the last time I saw you, and hear my difficulties, and help me if you can?

'After all, you are the only man whose good sense and honour I would trust in such a crisis of my life — the only friend before whom I would bare the secrets of my heart. Do come, and promptly.

'Yours, as ever, G. H.'

Of course Lucius complied. He left London early in the afternoon, and arrived at Stillmington towards evening. He found Geoffrey waiting on the platform, with much of the old brightness and youthfulness of aspect, but with a more thoughtful expression than of old in the candid face, a graver look about the firm well-cut mouth. They greeted each other in the usual off-hand manner.

'Uncommonly sweet of you to come, old fellow,' said Geoffrey. 'I ought to have run up to you, of course, only—only I've taken root here, you see. I know every post in the streets, every tree in the everlasting avenues that make the glory of this slow old town. But still I remain. You're looking fagged, Lucius, but bright as of old.'

'I have been working a little harder than usual, that is all,' replied Lucius, who was disinclined to speak of his new happiness yet awhile. It would be time enough to tell Geoffrey when the future lay clearer before him; and as he had somewhat ridiculed his friend's passion, he did not care to own himself a slave.

'Now, Geoffrey, what is the matter?' he asked presently, as they strolled slowly along one of those verdant avenues of lime and chestnut which surrounded the little gem-like town of Stillmington with a network of greenery. 'Still the old story, I suppose.'

'Yes, Lucius, the old story, with very little variation. She is here, and I can't tear myself away, but go dawdling on from day to day and hour to hour. Half-a-dozen times I have packed my portmanteaus and ordered the fly to take me to the station, and then at the last moment I have said to myself, "Why should I go away? I am a free man, and an idle one, and may just as well live here as anywhere else."'

'Ah, Geoff, that comes of your being without a profession.'

'It would be just the same if I were halfway towards the Woolsack—ay, if I were Lord Chancellor —I should only be torn in twain between my profession and my hopeless foolish love.'

'But how does it happen that she—Mrs. Bertram

—is still here? Are there perpetual concerts in Stillmington?'

'No; but after the little girl's illness, perhaps in consequence of that, she took a disgust for concert singing. She fancied the hurrying from place to place—the excitement caused by frequent change of scene—bad for her darling's health. Nor was this her only reason; she has often told me her own dislike of public life. So when the little girl recovered, Mrs. Bertram advertised for pupils in the local papers. The doctor, who had taken a great fancy to her, recommended her to all his patients, and in less than a month she had secured half-a-dozen pupils, and had taken nicer rooms than those in which you saw her. She has now a singing class three times a week. I hear them sol-faing when I pass the windows during my morning walk. There is even a little brass-plate on the door: "Mrs. Bertram, teacher of music." Imagine, Lucius, the woman I love to the verge of idolatry is obliged to put a brass-plate on her door and teach squalling misses, while I am wallowing in wealth.'

'A much better life for any woman than that of a public singer,' said Lucius; 'above all for—'

'Such a lovely woman as Jane Bertram. Yes, I agree with you. Who could see her and not adore her? But think, Lucius, how superior this woman must be to all the things which most women love, when she can willingly surrender professional success, the admiration of the public, even the triumph of her art, for the love of her child: and shut herself in from the world, and resign herself to lead a life as lonely and joyless as the life of a convent.'

'It proves, as you say, that the lady possesses a superior mind; for which I should have given her credit even without such evidence. But it appears that in her seclusion she has not closed her door against you; since you are so familiar with her opinions and her mode of life.'

'There you are wrong. I have never crossed the threshold of her present abode. On the very day you left Stillmington she told me in the plainest words, but with a gentleness that made even unkind words seem sweet, that she could receive no farther visits from me. "You have been very good," she said, "and in the hour of trouble such friendship as you have shown to me is very precious. But now the danger is past I can only return to my old position. It is my destiny to live quite alone; pray do not try to come between me and Fate.'

'You pleaded against this decision, I suppose?'

'With all the force of the truest passion that man

ever felt. I think I was almost eloquent, Lucius, for at the last she burst into tears; she entreated me to desist, told me that I was too hard upon her, that I tempted her too cruelly. How could I tempt her if she did not care a straw for me? These ambiguous phrases fanned the flame of hope. I left her at her command, which I dared not disobey; but I stayed in Stillmington.'

'You have stayed on all this time and seen no more of her?'

'*Pas si bête.* No, I have seen her and talked to her now and then. She is obliged to give her child an airing every fine afternoon. She has no maid here, and the mother and child walk out together. Sometimes, but not too often, for that would seem like persecution, I contrive to meet them, and join them in their ramble in one of the long avenues or across a breezy common; and then, Lucius, for a little while I am in Paradise. We talk of all manner of things; of life and its many problems, of literature, art, nature, religion, and its deepest mysteries; but of her past life she never speaks, nor of her dead husband. I have studiously refrained from any word that might seem to pry into her secrets, and every hour I have spent with her has served but to increase my love and honour for her.'

'You have again asked her to be your wife?'

'Over and over again, and she has refused with the same steadfast persistence, with a constancy of purpose that knows no change. And yet, Lucius, I believe she loves me. I am neither such a blockhead nor such a scoundrel as to pursue any woman to whom I was an object of dislike, or even of indifference. But I see her face light up when we meet; I hear the sweet tremulous tones of her voice when she speaks of the love she refuses to grant me. No, Lucius, there is no indifference, there is no obstinate coldness there. God only knows the reason which keeps us asunder, but to me it is an inexorable mystery.'

'And you have sent for me only to tell me this. In your letter you spoke of my helping you. How can any help of mine aid you here?'

'In the first place, because you are a much cleverer fellow than I am, a better judge of human nature, able to read aright much that is a mystery to me. In the second place, you, who are not blinded by passion, ought speedily to discover whether I am only fooling myself with the fancy that my love is returned. You know I was just a little inclined to be jealous of you the last time you were here, old fellow.'

'You had not the faintest reason.'

'I know. Of course not. But I was fool enough to grudge you even her gratitude. I don't mean to repeat that idiotcy. You are the only friend whose opinions I really respect. The common run of one's acquaintance I look upon as egotistical monomaniacs; that is to say, they have all gone mad upon the subject of self, and are incompetent to reason upon anything that has not self for its centre. But you, Lucius, have a wider mind; and I believe, your judgment being untroubled by passion, you will be able to read this mystery aright, to fathom the secret my darkened eyes have vainly striven to pierce.'

'I believe that I can, Geoffrey,' said Lucius gravely. 'But tell me first, do you really wish this mystery solved, for good or for evil, at the risk even of disenchantment?'

'At any hazard; the present uncertainty is unbearable. I am tortured by the belief that she loves me, and yet withholds her love. That if inclination were her only guide, she would be my wife. And yet she toils on, and lives on, lonely, joyless, with nothing but her child's love to brighten her dreary days.'

'There are many women who find that enough for happiness. But, no doubt, as your wife her existence might be gayer, her position more secure.'

'Of course. Think of her, Lucius, that loveliest and most refined among women, slaving for a pittance.'

'I do think of her, I sympathise with her, I admire and honour her,' answered the other, with unwonted earnestness.

'And yet you advise me against marrying her. That seems hardly consistent.'

'I have advised you not to marry her in ignorance of her past life. If she will tell you the secret of that past—without reserve—and you find nothing in the story to diminish your love, I will no longer say do not marry her. But there must be nothing kept back—nothing hidden. She must tell you all; even if her heart almost breaks in the telling. And it will then be for you to renounce her and your love; or to take her to your heart of hearts to reign there for ever.'

'I do not fear the test,' cried Geoffrey eagerly. 'She can have nothing to tell me that she should blush to speak or I to hear. She is all goodness and truth.'

'Have you ever asked for her confidence?'

'Never. Remember, Lucius, I possess her friendship only on sufferance. In a moment she may give me my irrevocable dismissal, forbid me ever to speak to her any more, as she has forbidden me to visit her. I could not afford to surrender even those occasional hours we spend together.'

'In that case why send for me? I thought you wanted to bring matters to a crisis.'

'Why, so I do. Yet at the thought of her anger I grow the veriest coward. Banishment from her means such unutterable misery, and to offend her is to provoke the sentence of banishment.'

'If she is as good and true as you believe, and as I too believe her to be, she will not be offended by your candour. She may have a confession to make to you which she could hardly make unasked; but which, once being made, might clear away all doubt, remove every impediment to your happiness.'

'You are right. Yes, I will hazard all. What is that old verse?

> "He either fears his fate too much,
>   Or his desert is small,
> Who dares not put it to the touch,
>   To gain or lose it all."

Just imagine my feelings on the twelfth, Lucius, when I thought of my collection of guns going to rust, and those Norwegian hills that I had made up my mind to shoot over this very August.'

'Bravely said, Geoff. And now I will do my uttermost to aid you. I think that I may have some small influence with Mrs. Bertram. Her gratitude exaggerated the trifling service I did her sick child. I will write her a letter; as your friend I can say much more than you could say for yourself. You shall deliver it into her hands, and then ask her, in the simplest, plainest words, to tell you whether she loves or does not love you; and, if she owns to caring for you a little, why it is she rejects your love. I think you will come at the truth then.'

'You will write to her!' cried Geoffrey aghast. 'You, almost a stranger!'

'How can I be a stranger when she thinks I saved her child's life? Come, Geoffrey, if I am to help you I must go to work in my own way. Give Mrs. Bertram my letter, and I'll answer for it, she will give you her confidence.'

Geoffrey looked at his friend with the gaze of suspicion. Yet, after entreating his aid, he could hardly reject it, even if the manner of it seemed clumsy and undiplomatic.

'Very well, I'll do it. Only, I must say, it strikes me as a hazardous business. Write your letter; but for heaven's sake remember she is a woman of a most sensitive nature, a most delicate mind! I implore you not to offend her.'

'I know more of her mind than you do,—by the light of psychology.'

'Very likely,' replied Geoffrey rather gloomily. 'But you haven't hung upon her words or studied her looks day after day as I have done. Psychology is an uncommonly easy way of getting at a woman's mind if you know much of her after a single interview. However, write your letter, and I'll deliver it. I can cut my throat if it makes her angry.'

'One does not cut one's throat at seven-and-twenty,' said Lucius coolly. 'And now, Geoff, if you have no objection, I should not be sorry to bend my steps towards your hotel with a view to refreshment. We seem to have wandered rather far afield.'

Geoffrey, in his desire for unrestrained converse with his friend, had led him away from the town, by a winding road that ascended a gentle hill; a wooded hill covered with richest green sward, whence they looked downward on the gentlemanlike town of Stillmington, with its white villas and spotless streets and close-cut lawns and weedless flower-beds, over which the sister spirits of order and prosperity spread their protecting wings. The respectable family hotel proudly dominated the smaller tenements of the High-street, its well-kept garden gaudy with geraniums, its fountain spirting mildly in the sunset.

'Come along, old fellow,' said Geoffrey; 'it was rather too bad of me to forget how far you'd travelled. I've ordered dinner for eight sharp; and hark, the clock of Stillmington parish church proclaims half-past seven, just time enough to get rid of the dust of the journey before we sit down. And after—'

'After dinner,' said Lucius, 'I'll write to Mrs. Bertram.'

'Then by Apollo, as old Lear says, I'll deliver the letter to-night. I couldn't afford to sleep upon it. My courage would evaporate, like Bob Acres's, before morning.'

Thus, with simulated lightness, spoke the lover, while strange doubts and gnawing fears consumed his heart.

END OF VOL. I.

LONDON:
ROBSON AND SONS, PRINTERS, PANCRAS ROAD, N.W.

www.ingramcontent.com/pod-product-compliance
Lightning Source LLC
Chambersburg PA
CBHW030012240426
43672CB00007B/919